THEY LET ME WRITE A BOOK!

HarperCollins*Publishers*
1 London Bridge Street
London SE1 9GF

www.harpercollins.co.uk

First published in New Zealand by HarperCollins*Publishers* 2015
First published in the UK by HarperCollins*Publishers* 2015

10 9 8 7 6 5 4 3 2

© Jamie Curry 2015

Jamie Curry asserts the moral right to be
identified as the author of this work

Front cover photograph by Sally Tagg
Back cover and internal photos courtesy of the author,
except pages 162, 176 and188 (bottom) by Sally Tagg
Illustrations by Matt Stanton, HarperCollins Design Studio
Cover and internal design by Anna Egan-Reid

A catalogue record of this book is
available from the British Library

TPB ISBN 978-0-00-815941-2
EB ISBN 978-0-00-815942-9

Printed and bound in Great Britain by
Clays Ltd, St Ives plc

MIX
Paper from
responsible sources
FSC C007454

FSC is a non-profit international organisation established to promote
the responsible management of the world's forests. Products carrying
the FSC label are independently certified to assure consumers that they
come from forests that are managed to meet the social, economic
and ecological needs of present and future generations.

Find out more about HarperCollins and the environment at
www.harpercollins.co.uk/green

THEY LET ME WRITE A BOOK!

JAMIE CURRY

with ALEX CASEY

HarperCollins*Publishers*

CONTENTS

actual monkey

INTRODUCTION

Hi! lol. Here Goes Nothing ...

'HOW AM I SUPPOSED TO START A WHOLE BIG BOOK WHEN I CAN'T EVEN START A VIDEO PROPERLY?'

HI, HELLO. HI THERE. HOWDY DO. OH LOOK,

I've ruined it already. I don't really know how to start a book. Look at me. How am I supposed to start a whole big book when I can't even start a video properly, as I'm sure you are well aware? I've decided to call this book *They Let Me Write a Book!*, because that's about how I am feeling right now, and I'm sure 'they' are feeling right now. Whoever they are. All out there united in wondering why on Earth this is all happening. Why have I been given the power over all of this blank paper? Why me? I ask that question every day.

When 'they' asked me to come up with a title, I imagined that I was an eight-year-old who had just been asked to write a book. Don't ask me why I chose eight, and didn't just go with nineteen like I am now. I think eight-year-olds have enough of a brain going to make decisions, but haven't lived long enough to let annoying life stuff get in the way of their impulses. So here I am, eight-year-old me, deciding what to call my book.

My first eight-year-old reaction, as has been the reaction of everyone around me, was THEY let ME write a BOOK?! So I thought I should run with that. Just to make it very clear from the very beginning: I'm as surprised as you are that all of this is happening.

If you have picked this book up in a public toilet, or if it was being used to prop up a desk in your office, you are probably feeling pretty confused right now. Allow me to introduce myself. I'm Jamie, I'm nineteen years old. I make videos on the Internet, and enough people watched them that they let me write a book. I know. I can't tell you what's going on with the world either. What is life?

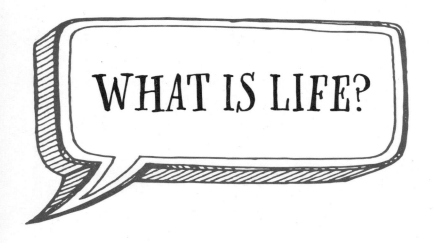

'JUST TO MAKE IT VERY CLEAR FROM THE VERY BEGINNING: I'M AS SURPRISED AS YOU ARE THAT ALL OF THIS IS HAPPENING.'

1

•••••••••••••••••••••••

That's Not
a Rocket:
Baby Me Calls
a Box a Box

'WELCOME TO JAMIE'S WORLD: I'M PUSHING THE TROLLEY BUT THERE'S NOBODY IN IT TO STEER.'

I THINK I HAVE A HANDLE ON MYSELF NOW, but I don't really remember when I first knew that I was a person. My earliest memory is probably of being at kindergarten, pushing around this special trolley that had a steering wheel in it. There was nobody inside it, so nobody was steering the wheel. That's not only my first memory, but my first of many memories where I have done something wrong and embarrassing. Welcome to Jamie's World: I'm pushing the trolley but there's nobody in it to steer. That's got to be a symbol of something for sure. What am I doing? Who am I steering? What's my plan of attack? Take notes, there will be a quiz at the end.

Invisible friends sitting in trolleys aside, I wasn't actually the most imaginative of kids. I don't even think that I had an imagination until I was about eight. The same age I picture myself being able to come up with this book title. Before eight, if you caught me jumping off a box, I'd be saying 'I'm jumping off this box' rather than 'I'm jumping off this rocket ship'. I called a box a box. I wasn't messing around with ideas and make-believe. But I was happy. I was probably the happiest kid of all time, which I'm sure was very annoying to everyone around me. Nothing has really changed since I was that little kid on a box. Now I just annoy people from a different kind of box.

'NOTHING HAS REALLY CHANGED SINCE I WAS THAT LITTLE KID ON A BOX. NOW I JUST ANNOY PEOPLE FROM A DIFFERENT KIND OF BOX.'

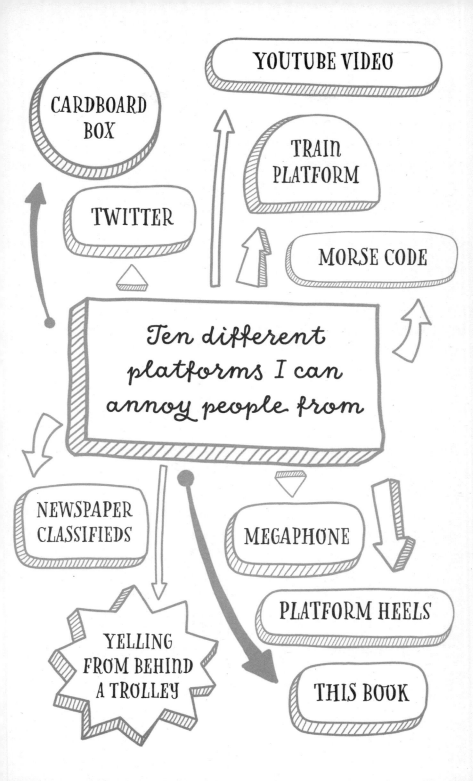

> ## DAD'S TAKE
> ### *Jamie on that big ball in the sky*
>
> 'I think Jamie has always had quite noticeable talents, even from a very young age. I always thought she was going to be a successful athlete. She was extremely coordinated, very good at juggling and doing all of those things. It was very telling that when she was a baby she would look up at the moon and say "ball".'

Although I may give off the 'oddball only child yelling about boxes' kind of vibe, I actually have a younger sister called Tayla. I know that she exists now — well, at least I'm pretty sure — but I don't remember her ever existing in my childhood. The only memory I have is of her as a baby, when she was chilling in one of those elastic baby rocker things. I would have to restrain myself from pinging it back and making her fling across the room. Aside from that, as far as I'm concerned I was pretty much an only child till I was about six. But don't tell my sister that. She was probably too busy orbiting the Earth on her post-pinged baby rocker anyway.

I was always good at getting what I wanted as a child.

'AS FAR AS I'M CONCERNED I WAS PRETTY MUCH AN ONLY CHILD TILL I WAS ABOUT SIX. BUT DON'T TELL MY SISTER THAT.'

Mum took me into a store and I picked up this Barney toy and wouldn't let it go. Mum had to buy it.

When I was about three, Mum took me to the shops with her. Big mistake. I latched on to a Barney soft toy that I found particularly fetching, and dragged it around the shop with me. Mum tried to get me to put it back so we could leave the shop. I wouldn't let it go. I tightened my grip like a vice and screamed and screamed. She was left with no choice but to buy me the Barney toy so we could leave the shop and get on with our lives. That's life lesson number one: seize onto what you want and never, ever let go of it.

Barney kidnappings aside, our family life is pretty normal. We like to celebrate Christmas in a big group and go on little holidays around the country. We come together in whatever Christmas house has been chosen by the powers that be that year (maybe Santa?). And then we'd have a big shindig that would always end in all of the little kids hiding from the drunk adults and giggling. The best Christmas present I ever got was a scooter when I was five years old. I still believed in the big SC (Santa Claus) back then. I wished so hard for that scooter, and good old Santa came through. Now I just get special car wash soap for Christmas. Oh man, I'm old, aren't I? Ever just go to sleep as a kid and wake up as an adult getting showered in car wash soap?

'NOW I JUST GET SPECIAL CAR WASH SOAP FOR CHRISTMAS. OH MAN, I'M OLD, AREN'T I?'

'MY MUM INSISTS ON USING THE SAME CAKE MOULD EVERY YEAR, WHICH SEEMS LIKE A RIP-OFF BECAUSE I KEEP GETTING BIGGER BUT THE CAKES STAY THE SAME SIZE.'

Sometimes over the holidays we go on family trips. Our last one was to the Gold Coast in Australia. We've been twice, actually. We just had so much fun the first time that we thought we'd do the exact same trip four years later. We're an original family. So we hit all the theme parks like Movie World and Dream World. When we went to the theme parks the first time, I was completely invisible. I could just run around, free to not go on any of the rides due to my crippling fear of heights. The dream holiday.

More recently, going back to the same theme parks has been a whole different ordeal. I had to hide myself from people, keeping my head down around anyone under the age of 18 — which is, unfortunately, almost everyone at a theme park. This must be how Mickey Mouse feels when he just wants to wander Disneyland in peace. Just kidding, I didn't just compare myself to the most famous and recognisable character in the world. There's no way they would publish that, right? You guys? Don't put that in.

As well as endlessly returning to the Gold Coast, our family likes to keep up birthday traditions. My mum insists on using the same cake mould every year, which seems like a rip-off because I keep getting bigger but the cakes stay the same size. Again, that's another perfect example of why eight is the ultimate age. Cakes are still huge for your tiny eyes. Mum would always ask us what colour we wanted the icing, and every single year the colour would come out weird. I asked for purple icing and I always got green. I got a mysterious dark blue cake for my birthday once. It's just better if you don't ask questions.

I love that tradition, almost as much as I love the Denny's tradition that follows. Every year I get to go to Denny's on my birthday and order bacon and eggs, curly fries and a grilled cheese. That's all you need in life: weird-coloured cakes and a huge Denny's banquet. I'm yet to finish my three-course Denny's birthday lunch in my nineteen years, but I've got at least three more tries before I die of heart disease.

I've never been trick-or-treating because my parents thought it was too dangerous — not like letting your daughter talk to ten million people on the Internet without a clue what she's doing or saying, and then even letting her write a book. I remember once we found some eyeliner and went nuts drawing rings around our eyes and filling in our lips. Our aunty let us sit in the back of her van and drove around with us ghouls just staring out the window at people. That one-off event was probably scarier for everyone else in our town than all the Halloweens put together.

So yeah, my childhood was pretty bog standard. Aside from the terrifying van window displays. Oh, and the magpies that would attack us when we went to the mailbox. There was nothing standard about that — the local magpies got so aggressive that we would have to wear helmets to

'I'VE NEVER BEEN TRICK-OR-TREATING BECAUSE MY PARENTS THOUGHT IT WAS TOO DANGEROUS – NOT LIKE LETTING YOUR DAUGHTER TALK TO TEN MILLION PEOPLE ON THE INTERNET.'

get the mail in the morning. Eventually, I domesticated a magpie of my own and called it Magz, but the rest of them were vicious creatures. I've been pecked in the head by magpies so many times, it's no wonder I've turned out like this.

Magpies or not, I still spent a lot of time running around outside. My sister and I would make up all sorts of pretty dangerous games to pass the time — there's not a heck of a lot to do in Napier, New Zealand. We would stand our trampoline on its side, cover it in soapy water and see who could climb up to the top the fastest. When it got really windy, we'd race outside with umbrellas and roller skates and let the wind drag us down the driveway like Mary Poppins. I'm surprised I didn't get more head injuries growing up ... or maybe I did ...

cute hat

fashion is kind of my thing

'WHEN IT GOT REALLY WINDY, WE'D RACE OUTSIDE WITH UMBRELLAS AND ROLLER SKATES AND LET THE WIND DRAG US DOWN THE DRIVEWAY LIKE MARY POPPINS.'

HOLY MOTHER

What is that face??!

2

•••••••••••••••••••••••••

My Double Life as a Sports Superhero and Amateur Hole-digger

'IT WASN'T UNTIL I GOT OLDER THAT I REALISED JUST HOW MEAN THOSE KIDS WERE TO ME, AND JUST HOW LONELY I ACTUALLY WAS.'

I DIDN'T HAVE MANY FRIENDS AT INTER-

mediate (that's middle school for anyone reading this outside New Zealand). I was made fun of because I was the sports girl of our school. The boys would ask me out and I'd agree and they'd be like 'haha' and run away. Turns out they were kidding. Joke's on them, I was definitely kidding as well. 100%. Taking the mickey. I hadn't picked out the outfit or cleared my calendar or anything. I hated intermediate, I lost a lot of confidence there. It wasn't until I got older that I realised just how mean those kids were to me, and just how lonely I actually was. I was odd, I had terrible social skills, but I didn't actually know. Until people started telling me, of course.

New Zealand Ice Skating Association Inc

Affiliated to the International Skating Union

Kiwi Skate

Certificate of Achievement

Beginner

Part 3/4

Instructor *Joe Palmer*

Paradice Skateschool

Dated 20/6/02 Signed

It was different to primary school where the sports people are like superheroes. I wasn't the cool girl any more — I was just the manic sports freak playing badminton, soccer, tennis, squash, and T-ball. I was honestly obsessed with sport; I even made the front page of the *Napier Mail* for being all-round sports champ of the world. That was my first taste of fame, my big beaming face in the paper with a sensational bowl cut.

I stopped doing this when I saw a weird kid in our class eating ice in the corner.

'YOUTUBE RUINED MY RIPPED MUSCULAR BODY – YOU GUYS OWE ME FOR THAT. I'LL ACCEPT PROTEIN POWDER SACHETS IN MY PO BOX.'

Don't know if I want to read this...

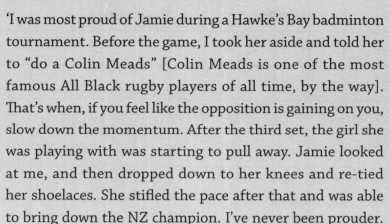

DAD'S TAKE
Sporty Jamie's shoelace strategy

'I was most proud of Jamie during a Hawke's Bay badminton tournament. Before the game, I took her aside and told her to "do a Colin Meads" [Colin Meads is one of the most famous All Black rugby players of all time, by the way]. That's when, if you feel like the opposition is gaining on you, slow down the momentum. After the third set, the girl she was playing with was starting to pull away. Jamie looked at me, and then dropped down to her knees and re-tied her shoelaces. She stifled the pace after that and was able to bring down the NZ champion. I've never been prouder. I think people need to know that side of her; she's made herself geeky but she's not as uncoordinated as she appears.'

Mum would race me around everywhere after school every day. I'd go from soccer training to tennis to whatever other sporting event was on. You should have seen me back then — I was so muscly. Then I just suddenly let myself go. Fitness doesn't matter as much to me any more, although I wish it did. I had to give it all up because of YouTube. Every weekend I'll be travelling around now. I'm so unfit now, even though I know that exercise is so important. I'm starting my new life on Monday, I swear. YouTube ruined my ripped muscular body — you guys owe me for that. I'll accept protein powder sachets in my PO Box.

Before YouTube

After YouTube

I was pretty oblivious to the rest of the world before high school. I just played sport all the time, and then I'd come home and bounce on the trampoline for hours or just dig holes. I'm talking literally about massive holes — there's a huge one in our backyard that still hasn't been filled in. I was basically a child-sized mole. I would dig all the way down and then back up so I could make a jump for my bike. Oh yeah, it could fit a bike by the way — it was legit. I dug stairs into the side of it, and slowly moved a whole heap of furniture down there. I'd chill out on my deck chair next to all this hoarded stuff. The hole was pretty much a self-contained apartment towards the end. Pity it didn't have a roof.

'THE HOLE WAS PRETTY MUCH A SELF-CONTAINED APARTMENT TOWARDS THE END. PITY IT DIDN'T HAVE A ROOF.'

'BRINGING A BALL
TO SCHOOL IS A
GREAT WAY TO
MAKE FRIENDS
IF YOU HAVE
NOTHING ELSE
TO OFFER.'

DAD'S TAKE
Jamie eats the whole pi

'In Jamie's first year at Sacred Heart school, part of her homework one night was learning about pi in maths. After school she had tennis practice at her local tennis club and her mum, Bronwyn, was running late. To fill in time at the tennis club, Jamie started reading up on pi.

A week later in class, the teacher asked if anyone could recall any of the numbers of pi. The class went silent. After a while, Jamie stood up and proceeded to recall the numbers 3.141592653589793238462643383279. I believe she had memorised up to thirty digits past the decimal point.'

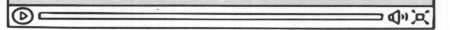

When I wasn't in my hole I remember eating my lunch by myself a lot during this phase of my life. It was pretty sad. I don't know what I did for fun when I spent all those lunchtimes alone. I used to play touch rugby sometimes. I'd bring a rugby ball to school and everyone knew I had it so that was my way of getting in with them. Bringing a ball to school is a great way to make friends if you have nothing else to offer. They see the ball and they're like, 'You can hang with us.' It doesn't matter how weird your bob cut is.

Living up to my fashion icon status

3

Please Don't
Bully the Poor
Kid in the
Cowboy Hat

'IT COULD HAVE BEEN THAT I WORE A COWBOY HAT FOR SEVERAL YEARS STRAIGHT ... BUT WE'LL NEVER REALLY KNOW WHY I STRUGGLED TO MAKE FRIENDS.'

EVERYONE I'M FRIENDS WITH NOW ALWAYS

teases me about what I used to be like. They all thought I was so weird, and they still remind me of that constantly now. I don't know what it was. Could have been the sportiness. Could have been that I didn't brush my hair for a year. It could have been that I wore a cowboy hat for several years straight … but we'll never really know why I struggled to make friends.

Jamie's tried and tested advice for social situation nerves

I was a really weird kid, and I've grown into a really weird adult. But I'm a child of the Internet, and the Internet is full of useful life hacks. I've assembled some of my tried and tested life hacks to combat nerves in social situations. Hopefully, they are helpful to you or anyone else you know cowering behind their customised cowboy hat.

Don't be a lone wolf, be a wolf pack

Don't isolate yourself from the situation by standing far away from everyone. If you stand next to a group of people that are talking, eventually they will bring you in if they are good people. Even if it takes months, years. Wait it out, be a magnet to them and eventually something's gotta stick.

Turn on your Chatty Cathy radar and pounce

Find the loudest person in the room and stand next to them; you'll at least get a healthy tan from their radiant confidence. And they'll talk to you, because they'll talk to anyone. You can practise saying things to them, and it won't matter if you muck up because they will not be listening to you 100% of the time.

Don't rush, slow it down to Chinatown

The world isn't actually going to explode if you don't say something witty, smart or cool in the next five seconds. Feel free to think long and hard before you say things. Take your sweet time talking if it's something that you need to do to feel more confident. People can wait, just don't take hours to ask someone what time it is. It will be way later by the time the question is over, and will just confuse everyone.

Find your feet, and when I say feet I mean voice

I know it might be cliché, but I've learnt it's really hard to write a book without at least a few making it in. The main thing, as we've been told since the cavemen wrote the first motivational quote on the wall, is BE YOURSELF. If you feel awkward, embrace the awkwardness. I'm still as awkward as that kid eating lunch alone, I've just learnt that nobody really cares. People are too involved in themselves most of the time anyway. Just let rip and see what happens.

~~~~~~

Oh yeah, so I guess we should talk about my weird hat thing. I wore hats constantly growing up, I had so many. Dad used to travel a lot and bring me baseball caps from around the world. My particular favourite was a cowboy hat that I used to wear absolutely everywhere. I would draw flowers on it, pin up the sides all different ways. I tried to seal off my drawings on the hat with superglue, which made it kind of chunky and even more dirty looking. Very chic. It was filthy anyway because I used to wear it in any and every situation. It became kind of my 'thing'. You know, Miley pokes her tongue out, Lorde has dark lipstick, Jamie has a decomposing cowboy hat. We're all the same.

'MILEY POKES HER TONGUE OUT, LORDE HAS DARK LIPSTICK, JAMIE HAS A DECOMPOSING COWBOY HAT.'

MUM'S TAKE
Even the hat can't fight the shade

'Jamie always wore hats, ever since she was about one year old. She didn't wear her hat to kindergarten one day and the teacher had to ask who she was. Everyone would say, "She's got such a pretty little face when she doesn't have a hat on."'

It was really tough feeling isolated when I was younger. But at the same time, I think it was good for me. The isolation gave me some fire. I became really determined to not be a loser at some point in my life. I used to always just sit there quietly and think about how these people won't really exist after I'm done with school. I just kept telling myself that one day I would grow up, move away and be better than them. I channelled all my energy and alone time into making something cool, and that was my ultimate payback. Now I'm making something cool and successful out of my weirdness, and I have them to thank for that. In a way.

If you are in this situation — just remember that bullies are the worst. Sit it out now, but give them ten years — they'll be sorry. Have a game plan, and get them back by being better than them. It's a pretty sweet long-term plan, you just have to commit.

'I CHANNELLED ALL MY ENERGY AND ALONE TIME INTO MAKING SOMETHING COOL, AND THAT WAS MY ULTIMATE PAYBACK.'

'HAVE A GAME PLAN, AND GET THEM BACK BY BEING BETTER THAN THEM.'

I always think about myself sitting there alone and feeling sad in my cowboy hat. It got me thinking that, if you ever find yourself alone for some reason and needing an activity, it might be fun to add some colour and cheer to your life. Sure, you can fiddle on your phone all you like — but what about a COLOURING-IN COMPETITION?

Colour in this glamorous picture of yours truly and see how fast the time passes. Why not even give it an Instagram and see who else has attempted this great artistic venture? It sounds kiddy, but colouring-in pages are actually making a huge comeback. Trust me, I know about what's cool and hip. I listen to Elton John and Third Eye Blind. You can trust me.

COLOUR ME IN!

4

•••••••••••••••••••••

Finally, a Comedy Star is Born (Jokes)

'MY STAGE DEBUT WAS AS A CREEPY LITTLE CAN-CAN GIRL, DESPITE HAVING NEVER DANCED IN MY LIFE.'

I HAD ZERO DESIRE TO PERFORM OR ACT

when I was younger. I was far too busy excavating my huge hole. At intermediate we were forced to do performing arts — they really tried to push it out of you back then. I absolutely hated the idea of it, but the second I got on stage I realised that it was actually really fun. That was my first big realisation that I could be a performer. Before that, I had only been in the big primary school performances where literally everyone is on stage. My stage debut was as a creepy little can-can girl, despite having never danced in my life. I hated it; it was very weird to be a five-year-old saloon-style can-can girl, coated in so much heavy make-up.

I never wanted to be a performer. I wanted to be a garbage man. I remember seeing the garbage men holding on

'I WENT HOME FROM SCHOOL AND TOLD MY MUM THAT I WAS GOING TO BE A GARBAGE MAN.'

Living the dream

to the truck with one arm and jumping off, and I thought that was so cool. Amongst all the kids that wanted to be astronauts and presidents, I went home from school and told my mum that I was going to be a garbage man. They were always fit and happy. I liked that. Still dreaming big to this day, I guess.

I remember when I first made a big group of people laugh at me. On purpose, I mean, not because I was wearing a rotten cowboy hat and sitting in a muddy hole. On feast days at church we would celebrate our saints, and each class would put on a performance for the school. The theme was TV shows, so I decided to be a hilarious presenter on *New Zealand's Got Talent*. It went really well, I absolutely slayed. That's when things sort of clicked for me, and people started telling me that I was funny.

During this time, I also started learning little magic

'I REMEMBER WHEN I FIRST MADE A BIG GROUP OF PEOPLE LAUGH AT ME. ON PURPOSE, I MEAN, NOT BECAUSE I WAS WEARING A ROTTEN COWBOY HAT.'

tricks with coins. I think those tricks helped me to learn how to perform, and gain a bit of confidence in front of a crowd. I would always whip them out at random times. People would get all excited about it and crowd around me. Universal truth: everyone loves magic. It's a great way to get attention; just yell 'Does anyone have a coin?' If you can't follow it up with anything, just run away. Free money.*

DAD'S TAKE
Jamie's bewildering magic

'On the badminton trips, Jamie would keep everyone entertained with magic and card tricks. She would do these simple tricks that would amaze me to this day — I still have no idea how she did them.'

The next year that we did our school production, I got my own bit in the play where I dressed in my nerd character costume. The same nerd that would later be in the 'White and Nerdy' video for all you old-school Jamie-philes out there. That nerd character, funnily enough, came from another production where the theme was YouTube. My

---

* This was a joke. Please don't steal from anyone, or at least don't blame it on me!

chosen YouTube clip was Kathy Beth Terry in *Last Friday Night*. When I saw the behind-the-scenes video for that, I couldn't believe how funny Katy Perry was. I wanted to be exactly like her.

The character was so dumb to me, but everyone thought it was hilarious. I saw them all in fits of laughter, and that's where people started to know me as 'Jamie the Funny Chick'. I found it easier to make more friends after I found the sense of humour that I liked. Everyone started to cotton on that I was weird as hell, but they liked me for it this time. I'm sure I've seen something on Instagram or Pinterest about how you have to like yourself before other people can like you, but I actually reckon it's true here.

JAMIE CURRY AS JAMIMA

'I FOUND IT EASIER TO
MAKE MORE FRIENDS
AFTER I FOUND THE
SENSE OF HUMOUR THAT
I LIKED. EVERYONE
STARTED TO COTTON ON
THAT I WAS WEIRD AS
HELL, BUT THEY LIKED
ME FOR IT THIS TIME.'

What do I think is funny?

On YouTube I started out doing a nerdy character, but I've now spiralled into over-sharing my thoughts, rambling and doing weird stuff in normal situations that makes me laugh. I tried hard to think about what makes me laugh the most, to try to figure out how I got this way. These are the things I came up with:

⇒ I still find physical humour very funny, I just try not to do it as much because pain. But watching Miranda Hart in *Miranda* fall over again and again is my favourite thing ever.

⇒ At the same time I like intelligent humour. I like a joke that gives you something to think about that is more clever than slapstick. I'm really trying to sound smart here but don't actually have any examples.

⇒ I actually hate Dad jokes. I hate all stupid jokes, which is funny because that's what my whole persona is built upon. I'm more complicated than you think. I confuse myself daily.

⇒ I like character comedy; I've recently become a huge fan of Kimmy Schmidt in *Unbreakable Kimmy Schmidt*. That's such a good show. I love seeing the characters on *Saturday Night Live* as well. They are funny, but it's even funnier when they break character. I love watching people trying not to laugh at their own jokes, it's my favourite thing. I'm a huge fan of doing it myself.

➠ I don't love puns — get away from me with your puns on my last name. Puns don't curry favour with me in the slightest. I'll have naan of that. See? Isn't it awful? You laughed, didn't you?

➠ I don't like stand-up comedy very much, especially when it's mostly just insulting other people and groups. I don't like nasty stuff like that, I don't think anyone should suffer for the purposes of your comedy. My rule is to only ever make fun of myself.

'I DON'T THINK ANYONE SHOULD SUFFER FOR THE PURPOSES OF YOUR COMEDY. MY RULE IS TO ONLY EVER MAKE FUN OF MYSELF.'

Probably the first Jamie's World ugly face picture.

Here's me thinking about how far I could ping Tayla across the room.

Mum clearly made us hold hands for this one. I can't remember the last time I hugged my sister, we just don't do that in our family.

I don't know where I am, what I'm doing, what I'm wearing, or what I'm thinking.

This is me at my Year 5 production. I'm the can-can girl with the ridiculous make-up on.

Who wants seconds? Clearly me, the little rat with two hands in the air.

This is my birthday at Denny's, staying true to tradition and flaunting my baller watch yo.

The start of my journey towards being a badminton champ. Until YouTube ruined it all, of course.

Winning cross country, a typical moment for me, to be honest.

I even wore the cowboy hat in the pool. Why is my tongue blue? You'll never know.

This is how I sleep with my duvet (that's Kiwi for 'quilt' or 'doona'): I wrap it over my head with a little breathing hole. I didn't realise I looked like a nun.

This photo displays everything about younger me. I was so happy, I didn't care what anyone thought of me, I was so weird. It was cold so I dressed like a marshmallow.

All you need in life is Zac Efron, a cat and a fluffy mullet.

I was cold, but I still wanted to be in the pool. Compromise is everything, people.

My eyes hadn't grown in yet.

The day that I got my guitar. If you look very closely, you'll see that I'm definitely not even playing a chord.

I was on the cover of the 'Napier Mail'. A lady at Subway recognised me and I couldn't believe it.

There's nothing wrong with playing pool in a fedora outside a gents' bathroom.

When my grandparents came to visit and never came over again.

5

·••••••••••••••••••••••·

Risky Tomato Sauce Heists at High School

'WE'D ALWAYS BE
DOING DUMB STUFF,
PERFORMING TO
EACH OTHER AND
TRYING TO MAKE
EACH OTHER
LAUGH.'

HIGH SCHOOL WAS WEIRD, BECAUSE I SUD-

denly had a big group of friends. We slowly all separated out as the years went on. By Year 12 (sixth form, senior, ten years after hole-sitting) I had two best friends — Grace and Jazz. We were the girls who sat around in the corner and didn't do anything. We'd hide from everyone and get kicked out of the common room daily. At lunchtime we would sit and talk, and I would put my puffer jacket on over my head and dance around. We'd always be doing dumb stuff, performing to each other and trying to make each other laugh.

I wasn't naughty, I was just really, really cheeky. I started to get busy as well with YouTube, and teachers would get more and more irritated with me. Teachers also hated my tiny finger skateboard that I would play with all day, confiscating it all the time. They just didn't understand the hard yards you have to put in to become the best finger skateboarder in the world. My favourite subject at high school was PE, as I still had a bit of old sports-mad Jamie in me. It was easy, fun, and I was good at it. I used to have the most incredible hand-eye coordination, but now that's all gone too. Thanks a lot, you guys, thanks a lot. I can hardly type properly any m07Prore.

I liked maths for a while, but I started to get very confused when they brought in all the letters. Towards the end, I didn't know if I was in English or math class. As it got harder, I did less and less work. I got kicked out of my statistics class because of this go-getter attitude. They

'THEY JUST DIDN'T UNDERSTAND THE HARD YARDS YOU HAVE TO PUT IN TO BECOME THE BEST FINGER SKATEBOARDER IN THE WORLD.'

'AT HIGH SCHOOL I GOT WORSE AT MATHS, BUT I GOT BETTER AT MAKING MY FRIENDS LAUGH AND GETTING AWAY WITH STUFF.'

moved me into a class for idiots after that. Sorry, not idiots. That's mean. All I'm saying is, someone asked me how to spell 'orange' when I was in there.

At high school I got worse at maths, but I got better at making my friends laugh and getting away with stuff. Now, I'm not saying this is good advice (again, see my shocked title before you take any advice from this book) but I got really good at forging signatures, and staying home from school. I can't think of a better example of my terrible evil skills than the great tomato sauce heist of modern times.

Before I can go on, I need to paint a picture of the kind of fussy eater I am. I am gold class fuss. I am fussier than any gluten-free, dairy-free, sugar-free person you will ever meet in your life. That will help you to really get a feel for the level of determination in this coming anecdote.

Food I don't like

Chicken, steak, macaroni cheese, any pizza that is not Hawaiian flavour, all sausages, sandwiches (no thank you, wet bread), fries (I can only eat curly fries), crisps — unless they're Pringles, spicy food (no curry to all you brainiacs out there), spaghetti bolognese, seafood.

Food I do like

Plain white rice, bacon and eggs, nachos (no sour cream allowed), spaghetti on toast, poached or boiled eggs, cereal.

Basically, if you are thinking of hosting a dream banquet for me, a breakfast buffet would be best.

Okay, so we're back in the room. Another condition of my strict kid-food-only diet is that I won't eat a meat pie unless it has tomato sauce with it (one of the more normal conditions). At high school one day I discovered that I didn't have any tomato sauce for my pie at lunchtime. This would not do, I would physically gag if I had to go through with this sauce-free. So I got scheming.

I immediately lied to my art teacher that I had to leave school for an orthodontist's appointment. I signed off the note as my dad, but then she told me she was going to give the school office a call to confirm. Obviously, she called the office and there was no message from my dad, because of course the appointment didn't exist. But I didn't give up there, I was not about to eat a sauce-free pie. I'm not a peasant.

'I WAS NOT ABOUT TO EAT A SAUCE-FREE PIE. I'M NOT A PEASANT.'

'DON'T BE NAUGHTY
IN FRONT OF
TEACHERS, JUST BE
SNEAKY WITH IT.
MAKE THEM TRUST
YOU, AND THEN
ABUSE THAT TRUST.'

While the teacher was calling the office, I secretly rang my dad. I told him that I had got my period suddenly and needed to come home, and that he needed to call the office and tell them I had an orthodontist's appointment because I was very embarrassed. Obviously, any time you put dads and periods together he's going to want to nip that in the bud as fast as possible. So he rang the office, and I went up the road to buy tomato sauce for my pie. I came back straight away and ate it, a local hero.

Jamie's forged note template

Here's a life hack: have both of your parents' signatures on lock during high school. I learnt both of them perfectly, but you can also just make friends with the kid who has really flash handwriting. They'll write the notes for you and then you can sign them. I used it to get out of work all the time. Don't be naughty in front of teachers, just be sneaky with it. Make them trust you, and then abuse that trust. That's the worst advice in the world. Welcome to the worst advice book in the world. I'm sorry to teachers everywhere.

It seemed selfish of me to brag about my forgery talents, so I thought I would share the gift with you. Below I have created a note template that you should feel free to tear out and use. In trouble with your parents? Need some more time to finish that school project? Want a day off work to watch *CSI* on the couch and eat waffles? Just fill in the blanks and watch your problems melt away.*

To whom it may concern,

Please excuse _____
from doing _____
today. He or she is feeling particularly
under the weather and needs a day of rest to
recover.

Thank you for your consideration,

_____

(Mum or Dad of _____)

* Please note that your problems might not melt away after using this. For example, I used mine to try to get out of writing this book. Look where we are now.

you're welcome :)

Reinventing the wheel: a quick zoom through driving

I love driving, I got my licence as soon as I could during high school. I am officially the best driver and the worst driver at the same time. I've never actually crashed. I mean I did once, but I've never *crash* crashed. I just like to throw the car around a bit. I can be quite heavy-footed when I want to be. Even before I was old enough, my dad would sneakily let me drive down our rural road as a small child. This gal has got a need for speed — ever since that early trolley at kindergarten I told you about. I'm confident that I've been on every type of wheels — chopper, scooter, roller skates. Unicycle.

You heard me, I ride a mean unicycle. Nobody ever believes me when I say I can. I'm still not sure why I decided to get into unicycling, but it seems to have really cemented my modern-day Internet clown vibe. When I was younger I was just completely obsessed with conquering things that I didn't know how to do. I ordered a unicycle online and spent every night in the garage trying to ride it. It took me a week. It's really, really hard.

As soon as I got my learner's licence I drove heaps and nailed all my tests on the first time. I am very, very skilful. Why am I boasting so much? I don't know — but it's my book and I'll do what I want. During my test I actually failed to parallel park and drove 50 km per hour in a 30 km per hour zone. But I still passed. This might sound like boasting again (and it is) but I think the testing lady really liked me. That would be my main driving tip: tell your testing instructor hilarious jokes and be exceptionally charming the entire time. They will be laughing so hard that they won't notice when you drive off a cliff.

'TELL YOUR TESTING INSTRUCTOR HILARIOUS JOKES AND BE EXCEPTIONALLY CHARMING THE ENTIRE TIME. THEY WILL BE LAUGHING SO HARD THAT THEY WON'T NOTICE WHEN YOU DRIVE OFF A CLIFF.'

Favourite bands/artists:

The 1975, Haim, One Direction. I'm not ashamed of this last one — Elton John.

Most played songs:

'Loyal' — Chris Brown
'Stay with Me' — Sam Smith
'I'm a Mess' — Ed Sheeran
'Poison and Wine' — Civil Wars
'Atlas' — Shannon Saunders
'Heart Out' — The 1975
'Stay High' — Tove Lo (Hippie Sabotage Remix)
'How It's Gonna Be' — Third Eye Blind
'Borderline' — Tove Styrke

0:00   4:00

During high school I went to my first school ball. And guess what I found out? I hate school balls a lot. Here's my advice for getting ready for your school ball or prom: just don't go. The first time I went to a school ball I spent so much money on horrible uncomfortable things because I thought that's what you had to do. I had the worst high heels that I couldn't even walk in. What even are high heels? Who came up with that disaster of an idea? A human foot is not supposed to bend like that, we are all about that flat foot life. I took my shoes off within five minutes at my first ball.

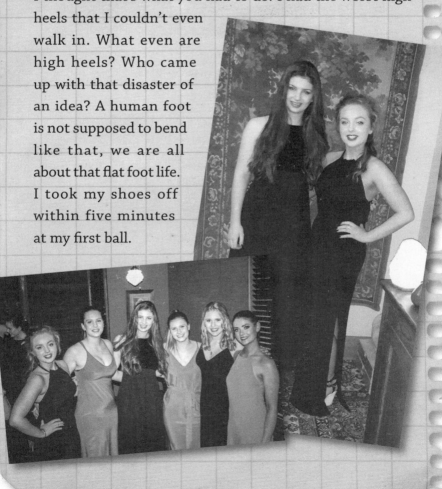

'WHAT EVEN ARE HIGH HEELS? WHO CAME UP WITH THAT DISASTER OF AN IDEA?'

> ‘MY FRIENDS BOOKED THEIR HAIR AND MAKE-UP 40 YEARS IN ADVANCE. I WAS JUST GETTING MY COUSIN TO COME OVER AND THROW SOME GLITTER AT MY FACE.’

My friends all got their dresses ordered real early, and booked their hair and make-up 40 years in advance. I was just getting my cousin to come over and throw some glitter at my face. My dress still hadn't arrived the day before the ball, and all my friends were freaking out about it. I didn't really care if my ball dress came or not, I was just going to rock a poncho or something. Then my friend Grace lent me her mother's 1950s vintage couture gown from Paris, so I wore that.

I didn't take a date in the second year either, which was so much better. Like, I can't even describe how freeing it was. The first year I took a guy I didn't know that well, and just had to make the most awkward chat with him all night long. Who would volunteer for that kind of torture?

I tried to avoid relationships at all costs during high school, actually, even though there were people literally bashing down my door to date me (none, there was none). I just got so sad seeing all my awesome friends get heartbroken again and again. Plus, my town was so small it just got very awkward, ended up with a lot of guys to avoid. I had fun, but dating was not for me. It's absolutely fine if it's not for you either. Don't stress too much, you aren't missing out on anything.

Jamie's top five celebrity crushes

Just because I'm not big on relationships, doesn't mean that I don't have fake celebrity relationships in my head. This might alarm you all, but Channing Tatum isn't on this list. If you watch my videos, you'll know that I used to talk about him a bit. I don't know where the Channing thing came from. I used him a few times for some memes when he was a real big thing, and then once or twice in my early videos.

Everyone then assumed he was my only guy crush. I started getting sent all these cardboard cut-outs in the mail, which made our postman think I was a total creep. The local newspaper issued me an apology when he got married, it was insane. I don't even care about him. Again, Channing, I'm not obsessed with you. Stop calling me, it's embarrassing for everyone. Here are my real fake boyfriends:

Zac Efron

Who doesn't like Zac Efron?! Even my dad likes Zac Efron. I've been a fan since *High School Musical*. He was one of my first celebrity crushes, and still is.

Justin Bieber

I have stuck with Bieber through thick and thin. I have faith.

I like his tattoos, and he has good hair and good fashion. Even his bad stuff isn't that bad — my male friends do bad stuff on a regular basis. I mean, I wouldn't wee in a mop bucket personally, but what person hasn't done something stupid like that? He's a teenage boy with $200 million dollars, something has got to go weird.

Kellan Lutz

Look, I just think he's cool. Just look at his little eyes! He has a nice smile and he is buff as hell.

Nick Jonas

Everyone has to choose one fantasy Jonas Brother to have. Joe does funny things with his hair. Kevin is married. So Nick is by far the best. Nick got himself sorted physically, and now he's making some really good music. A winning combo, and I am ... jealous.

Dave Franco

This is weird, but I had a dream last night that Dave Franco died and I was watching his brother James crying over his grave. I don't know why I was at the cemetery — obviously the family only wanted his most beloved there for the burial. This joke has gone too far. Everyone touch wood right now for Dave Franco. I just remembered how he died as well — he was having a cigar and it blew up in his face. I got that from an episode of *CSI*. Weird, sorry for bringing the mood down. I guess we should all stop smoking cigars. Anyway, he's hot and funny and still very much alive.

~~~~~~

I had the best time at the ball in my last year. I realised that chilling out is the most important thing in the world. It's only one night, focus on having fun with your friends. Remember that nobody cares about your appearance as much as you do, they are all too worried about themselves. To be honest, I did look really, really great though.

'REMEMBER THAT NOBODY CARES ABOUT YOUR APPEARANCE AS MUCH AS YOU DO, THEY ARE ALL TOO WORRIED ABOUT THEMSELVES.'

Presenting: one comically short beauty section

As you can probably tell by the things I have said on the topic already, and my stunningly glamorous high-fashion style — I am a guru in all things beauty.

ESSENTIAL MAKE-UP TIPS

Put it on your hands.
Put it on your face.

ESSENTIAL HAIR TIPS

Straighten it, if you want

But obviously you don't have to. My hair is secretly really frizzy, but nobody would know from my videos. They don't expect it to be a nightmare and then I rock up to a photo-shoot with a giant shrub growing out of my head.

Put stuff in it, if you want

I sometimes plop some potion onto my hair that's supposed to make it not turn into a frizzball, but it doesn't actually work. If it works for you, go for it.

Dye it, if you want

People always ask me if I dye my hair, and I have to tell you that it is 100% natural. I don't like my chances of colouring my own hair, if my mother's icing colour mix is anything to go by ...

ESSENTIAL SKINCARE TIPS

Wash your face

Cleansing with warm water is pretty much the only skincare thing I do every day. Wait till you hear how many times I wash my phone — it's lazy by comparison.

Occasional burn-your-face-off face mask

I recently started using a face mask for the first time. Can I be honest? It burns. Is it supposed to burn the skin that much? I think face masks are actually trying to literally burn a layer off your face so you have a whole new face afterwards. Prove me wrong.

ESSENTIAL FASHION MUST-HAVES

Whatever is comfortable.
Whatever is weather appropriate.

THEY LET ME WRITE A BOOK!

Brace yourself: a brief lesson in dentistry by Jamie Curry

To be honest with you, the cosmetic area that I probably have the most experience in is orthodontistry. As you'll see in some of my older videos, I had braces on my teeth for two years. And I hated every minute of it. It's not even over — I still have a hunk of metal sitting in my mouth now. I don't know what's tooth and what's robot at this stage.

I never smiled when I had braces, which is why I look so sad and angry in almost all of my teenage photos. That's also why I dressed so weird, just by the way, to distract from the braces. I knew what I was doing, I am a master of distraction. My braces were the bane of my existence, they were so painful that I remember wanting to get a hammer and just whack them off. Teeth and all.

Good things about having braces:

Nothing, except I suppose my teeth look exquisite now.

Bad things about having braces:

They hurt.
They are annoying.
The wire always breaks at the worst times.

You can't eat anything without it getting stuck in the wire forever.

You dribble a lot. Like, A LOT.

To all you brace-faces out there like me, I would say persevere. Hang in there, and just think about how good your teeth will look after your teeth are released from their tiny metal jail. Adapt your diet, eat soft food, and brush your teeth as much as you can. Accept that there's nothing you can do about your dribbling, but relax in the knowledge that you will never dribble as embarrassingly as I did. I dribbled in a video in front of ten million people. You'll be fine.

〜〜〜〜

Leaving high school was the biggest anti-climax of all time. At our graduation ceremony, each leaving student got given a rose. No certificates, no diplomas, no high-fives. Just an already dying rose. I was at school for twelve years of my short life, and all I had to show for it was a rose that I threw out the next day. It was like some dark, mutated version of *The Bachelor*.

The only diploma I have ever received, and will ever receive.

Everyone was crying and carrying on heaps, but I felt ready to leave high school. Me and my friends left the school gates the second the ceremony was over, and that was us finished. I hate having awkward goodbyes with people I didn't even know that well. I also had other things planned, it wasn't like I was leaving to go into nothing. Although, doing nothing sounds really nice sometimes. I had spent my last year of school organising my YouTube life for the moment I got to leave, so I was really excited to get amongst it.

'I WAS AT SCHOOL
FOR TWELVE YEARS
OF MY SHORT LIFE,
AND ALL I HAD
TO SHOW FOR IT
WAS A ROSE THAT
I THREW OUT THE
NEXT DAY.'

43

SUBSCRIBE FOR MORE

@THEJAMIESWORLD

JAMIESWORLD.COM

6

The Unexpected
Yet Natural
Birth of
Jamie's World

'EVERYONE TOLD ME THAT I SHOULD MAKE A PAGE, AND CALL IT JAMIE'S WORLD AS A JOKE. WE WERE TOTALLY KIDDING AROUND ABOUT THE WHOLE IDEA.'

SO, I SUPPOSE WE SHOULD TALK ABOUT

Jamie's World, my YouTube channel and Facebook page that got us all into this hot mess in the first place. I was going to try to do the whole book without it but, to be honest, I'm out of juice already.

A month or two after I had starting doing the iconic nerd character, we were talking at soccer training about this girl that had made a random Facebook page. She had a thousand likes. Everyone told me that I should make a page, and call it Jamie's World as a joke. We were totally kidding around about the whole idea. I made it, and two or three weeks later I was up to thousands of likes.

I remember being so stoked with getting 306 likes. Then it was 1000. Then it was 10,000. Then it was 100,000. Then

'NOW THE PAGE IS AT TEN MILLION, AND I THINK IT'S SAFE TO SAY THAT THINGS HAVE GOTTEN OUT OF HAND."

it was 100,000 a month. Everyone was like, what? Now the page is at ten million, and I think it's safe to say that things have gotten out of hand. But, another reminder that if you get enough likes on Facebook, they'll let you write a book.

The lawnmower 'White and Nerdy' video was the first video on my YouTube, dancing to 'Beauty and the Beat' was the first one on Facebook. Before the videos, I just posted a lot of stupid memes making ugly faces. That was fine in real life because my hideous faces would be so extreme that nobody would be able to recognise me. Once my videos started going out, I got recognised way more because I actually started to look like me. I couldn't hide behind the double chins and rubbery faces any more. Unless I constantly did shark face all day every day, but who wants to see that?

Once I realised that a lot of people were following me, I always tried to be consistent with my uploading. I remember in Year 11 we had to go on a retreat to get confirmed into our church. While I was getting confirmed, I was also trying to get confirmed by the YouTube world (which is pretty much a church in itself). We went away for a week or two to a camp, learned about God and picked a new middle name — all that normal stuff. I was so worried about YouTube that I pre-recorded some videos to go up while I was away.

I still find it hard to believe that so many people are watching me. My whole sense of humour has changed quite a bit. I used to be really into hurting myself. Not in a serious way, like the banana peel way. Now I'm trying to use my words more, as you can probably tell at this stage with the whole book thing. I've upgraded to Final Cut Pro to edit now, which is a step up from iMovie. Apart from that, I'm still operating with zero plan and zero clue.

DAD'S TAKE
Jamie strikes an Internet chord

'When Jamie's World started, I knew she had stumbled upon something big. She struck a chord with people, she's herself and she's relatable.'

MUM'S TAKE
Jamie: the maniac on the lawn

'We started watching her record her things, and they were funny as. She didn't mind that the neighbours were watching. You're going to post it to thousands of people, what do you care about one person who is wondering why you are running around like a maniac on the lawn?

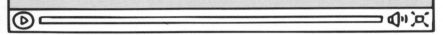

I try to stay away from the typical trendy tag videos as much as possible. A few times I've done things like 'The Whisper Challenge', which I still feel a bit bad about. It feels like a betrayal to you guys, and I think it's a lazy way out for a lot of YouTubers. I much prefer to do original ideas, and just talk to the camera. That's where the real weirdness comes out. Keep it real, keep it unplanned. I still have no idea what I'm doing to this day.

I normally think about my videos for a few days, and sometimes I'll just sit down, turn the camera on, and see what comes flying out of my mouth. I'll generally film for around half an hour, and then edit for four or five hours. It's the editing where the magic really happens. Can I call it magic? Sure, why not. Yer a wizard, Curry. Here are some of my 'production notes', also known as very vague bits of dialogue with little set description and shot direction so that only I can understand it. It's a bit like the Da Vinci Code, except nobody on Earth would want to read it. Let alone print it in a book. Oh, wait ...

5 July 2015, 9:43 am

Scene: out by trampoline

"hello"
Hi
"what's your name"
my name? My names Jamie Curry
"so what do you do"
I entertain people really.
"how do you do that?"
I ride things. Why does everyone laugh when i say that?

I ride scooters, ripsticks, bikes, unicycles, tricycles anything really yeah I'm really talented.
"how long have you been riding?"
I've been riding since I was born yeah. I came out of my mother womb on a bike. It's true yeah a little baby bike.

I think I'm fun. I'm adventurous and smart and pretty and stuff so i want to put some content on the internet that's truly inspiring and encourages people to basically be like me because I'm perfect. I also want a PO box so people she send me stuff yeah

so yeah basically i'm just gonna ride my bike down this mountain

Scene: walking bike to start

"are you nervous"
No only losers get nervous. I'm not a loser. I'm a winner

leaning against bike and it falls over

"are you alright?"
yeah I'm fine. Did you get that on camera? can you delete it?

Scene: at top of hill while sitting on bike

So I'm going to go straight down there. Do you wanna go set up over there. I want you to get a real good shot because I'm not doing this twice

rides hill

Scene: Pushing bike up hill

That was great. Really happy with that. This hills a bit of a bugger though

'IF YOU EVER MEET MY SISTER IN REAL LIFE, DON'T CALL HER "JAMIE'S SISTER". SHE'LL SCRATCH YOUR EYES OUT.'

My favourite videos of my own are ones that I have done with my sister, Tayla. She hates it so much, it brings me great delight. I literally have to pay her sometimes to appear in them. She hates the attention, but she's also got all these followers because of me. Even after changing her name on Instagram she's still got 60,000 followers. Don't try to find her, or follow her, she'll get angry like The Hulk. If you ever meet my sister in real life, don't call her 'Jamie's sister'. She'll scratch your eyes out.

My least favourite videos are impossible to find now, because I've deleted them all. I deleted one recently because I realised my breathing was really heavy through my braces. I sounded like Darth Vader after he's walked up seven flights of stairs. It's hard because these terrible videos still get about one million views before I delete them. I'm still not embarrassed very easily, I think people like watching me make a fool of myself and not caring about anything. Apart from that disgusting breathing, that was just too much.

Embarrassing moments

I'm sure I've had lots of embarrassing moments, but at the time I didn't know they were embarrassing. I think every moment of my life could be counted as an embarrassing moment, but here are some that stick out in my mind right now:

1 When I was about thirteen years old I was playing in badminton competitions with sixteen-year-olds. Because I was being my cool natural self, I was wearing track pants over my shorts. When I was getting ready to go on the courts, I whipped off my track pants thinking I could step out in my shorts. More than just my shorts came off. In front of everyone there. I actually imploded. I'm not making that story up, I really wish that I was.

2 One time at intermediate Dad yelled, 'Bye, Jamie, I love you!' I nearly died at that. I had just got out of the car to go to school when he yelled it from the window. I turned

around like, 'Whose dad is that?!' It was exactly like the start of every 'new kid at school' movie, and was not cool in the slightest. I'm still plotting my revenge as to when I'll do it to him.

3 Me and my cousin used to make up heaps of dances. I entered one dance in the talent show with her, but she couldn't make the performance for some reason. We normally would share the moves but I decided to stick it out and go solo with the same routine. My teacher rang my mum and actually said, 'Jamie's entering a dance into the talent show — are you concerned?' Turns out she should have been. I spent half the dance just bopping my head, waiting for my ghost partner to finish her moves.

4 When I got on stage at that same talent show, the host asked me to introduce myself. I said, 'Hi, my name's Jamie Curry and I'm going to be dancing to a song called "Jamie Curry".'

5 For everything else, see every photo of me ever taken before the age of twelve. Oh, and every photo taken after the age of twelve. A picture paints a thousand words … we'd run out of room if I went through them all.

I like being embarrassing, because I know you guys like that. Because you're embarrassing too, everyone is. There's no point pretending that you are perfect, because you will trip over, say the wrong word or dribble soon enough. I like to

'IT'S ALWAYS
BEEN A GOAL
OF MINE TO
LOOK AS UGLY
AS POSSIBLE ON
THE INTERNET.'

imagine that you guys out there are just a big group of like-minded Jamies. Let's all just dribble together. No wait, that came out wrong, I'm so sorry.

~~~~~~

I wish I had someone to look up to when I was younger who didn't fit in and didn't take themselves too seriously. A lot of my audience do it too now, and send me photos of themselves not looking pretty and stuff. That's cool to me, I never would have done that when I was thirteen. None of us is perfect. I think the younger that we learn that, the better. I wouldn't have spent so long sitting alone if I had known that it was okay for me to be myself.

It's always been a goal of mine to look as ugly as possible on the Internet. That was a big meme trend about who could look the ugliest, which was a cool backlash to the competition for hottest profile picture. (Is that a real thing? It seemed like a real thing.) That's where I made my Internet bread and butter, through looking as bad as possible. I still don't care about looking pretty. I take selfies, but I would honestly prefer not to. My Instagram is a total mess, but people like seeing photos of my face for whatever reason. I just wing it, I look like an idiot in selfies all the time. Actually, take an ugly selfie and send it to me right now, we're all hot messes together. Here's mine:

SHARE SHARK FACE!! ← ——— I'm sorry

Ten ways to hide a double chin

1   If you are Skyping someone, lie down on your bed and put the duvet directly over your double chin.

2   Wear a motorcycle helmet at all times — you can't see your chin at all then. Or your face.

3   Spend all your time with your chin resting on your hand; it will disguise the doubler and make you look thoughtful and wise.

4   Wear a really big turtleneck — thank goodness they have come into fashion again so I can really let my chin go this winter.

5   A simple scarf goes down a treat any season, and will make you look like a high fashionista with just the one chin. Just don't go riding in a top-down convertible because that could become chin mania.

6   Tie up your hoodie really tight around your whole head. Just leave your nose and mouth out for the old breathing and talking.

7   If you have your cat, just rest your cat there.

8   Try really hard to grow a beard.

9   Tell everyone that it's not your chin, you are just looking after it for a friend. They will see how kind and charitable you are.

10 Wear a cape with a cool collar — it won't hide the chin but it will distract people into thinking you are an off-duty superhero.

Or, you can just embrace it. Chins are just the chapters in the rich book of your neck's life. Just like this book. This book is brought to you by chins.

Favourite things

People always ask me about my favourite things, but I actually have no clue what to tell them. I don't like a lot of stuff. I don't have a lot in my room. If you were to see my room, it's pretty much empty. Like a guest bedroom with a permanent guest. I'm not kidding. In fact, I'm confident I could start a new life today and I wouldn't need to bring anything with me. But I thought long and hard about it for you, and here are my favourite things.

Sneakers

I like sneakers, but I only have one pair at a time. I'm not like Kanye or anything, more like a thrifty grandma. I like putting sneakers on, they are always so comfortable like a very thick, colourful, second skin. When you are wearing sneakers you can dress in running gear and everyone thinks you are super fit. I can go to the shops when I look like a hillbilly, and people just think you have been for a run. I just grab my chocolate and get out of there quick smart. You didn't see anything, I'm so speedy and fit and not eating chocolate in my car outside.

Plain ChapStick

ChapStick has to be on this list. I have three on the go at all times. There'll always be one in my pocket, one in my bedroom and one in my car. Give me just the plain vanilla flavour, no glitter or special flavours or anything. Just the old lady one, that will do me fine.

Nice mattress

I recently bought a new mattress and it's just really lovely. It's got a cover and everything. I spent ages looking for it. It's firm, but has a layer of squishy stuff. So it's hard, but it's soft. A very complex mattress. I know what you're thinking, how old is this girl?! I'm 87, and I'm having the best nights' sleep of my life.

Bacon and eggs

The only thing I like eating all day, every day. If you take me anywhere for dinner, don't scream when I ask for the breakfast menu. It's just how I roll, mad deep with brother bacon and my poached egg sisters. As I said earlier, every year on my birthday we go to Denny's and I order curly fries, a grilled cheese sandwich and bacon and eggs. I've never been able to finish it all, not in my 87 years on this Earth.

Xbox

I'm not materialistic, but I guess I like my Xbox. I don't even play it, I just like knowing that it's there. I play Call of Duty, Grand Theft Auto and Skate 1, 2 and 3. Actually just 2 and 3; 1 is real bad. But again, I could live without it. I'm rethinking my entire life. Maybe I'll become a Buddhist.

See? I'm not really attached to anything, not a lot has changed since I was little. I'd be happy with a hole in the ground — just make sure there's a ChapStick in there.

'I'D BE HAPPY
WITH A HOLE
IN THE GROUND
– JUST MAKE
SURE THERE'S
A CHAPSTICK IN
THERE.'

HA no thx

7

●●●●●●●●●●●●●●●●●●●●●●●●●

Dealing With
My Cool Life
Online

'I'M AN (CRINGING AS I WRITE THIS) "INTERNET CELEBRITY" WHO STRUGGLES TO DO EVEN THE SIMPLEST TASK ONLINE.'

THIS MAY COME AS A SHOCK TO YOU, SO I'LL

give you a moment to sit down. Put down your hot drinks and stop operating heavy machinery. Here it comes.

I don't know how to use the Internet.

That's right. I'm an (cringing as I write this) 'Internet celebrity' who struggles to do even the simplest task online. The truth is that, outside of uploading and sharing my videos, I don't actually spend a lot of time on the Internet. I'll do a tweet or a 'gram and then I'll put my phone down and do something else. The only exception is if I'm in a situation where I feel awkward — then Instagram is suddenly my best friend.

I don't actually know what I do when I'm not on the Internet. I'm not digging holes any more, but I just enjoy

'MOST OF THE TIME I'M JUST SITTING AND STARING AT A WALL LISTENING TO THE PHONE RING WHILE I PLAN WORLD DOMINATION IN MY HEAD.'

life away from the computer and phone sometimes. My friends all hate me because I never reply to their texts, and my agents hate me because I never reply to emails. Most of the time I'm just sitting and staring at a wall listening to the phone ring while I plan world domination in my head. Normal, I know.

The only website I spend a lot of time on is Tumblr. That's it. I follow a lot of fashion blogs, believe it or not, I like to just drool over all of the pretty photos. I am all about re-blogging other people's stuff on Tumlbr, I wouldn't even know how to do any of my own posts. Smart, I know.

I have stopped watching most other YouTubers now, I don't really have time. I watch the smaller ones, I occasionally watch Grace Helbig, because I love everything about her. I like watching Troye Sivan sometimes just to see what he's up to. It's so hard to keep up now, I don't know how you guys do it. I try to avoid obsessing over other people too much, I save that for my real life. And Channing. That's a joke, Channing, put the bunch of dozen red roses down. It's never going to work out between us.

My biggest fan

weird to be next to these two on tour!!!

My favourite TV shows

You'd think I might be at another type of screen when I'm not on the Internet, but I don't actually watch a whole lot of TV either. I suppose I should pay attention to it, it is like YouTube's grandma who just won't go away. She's just there, sitting silently in the corner of everyone's lounge. When I was little, my mum used to use TV as an evil tool to send me to sleep, and I think I never really got over it. Even today, if you play the opening of *Teletubbies*, I'll be snoozin' within four seconds. Here's two of my all-time favourite TV shows:

CSI

I'll never flick through channels, I always just record hours and hours of all the *CSI* franchises, *NCIS* and anything else with that combination of letters in the title. I think these sort of crime shows are always so good and the writing is so clever. You'd think I'd be able to figure out who did it by now — but I still get shocked by the twists and turns. Spoiler alert: it's nearly always the garbage man.

Keeping Up with the Kardashians

I love the Kardashians. I hate when people are mean to them and say they have no talent. They have so much talent, Kris Jenner is a branding goddess. They are really interesting characters to watch, even though they aren't movie stars or anything. I always swap between Khloe and Kim for my favourite, but I think they are all cool. And Caitlyn Jenner is obviously amazing, what she is doing for the transgender community is so huge and brave. To have a well-known role model will be incredible for young transgender people. The family were all understanding and supportive, I really think the world can learn more from the Kardashians than just how to contour really well.

Trolls and haters

Another big part of life online is dealing with a tsunami of haterade, which I have learnt how to confidently surf all the way to the sandy shores of 'I don't give a hoot' bay. There was a dude who messaged me years ago saying, 'Kill yourself and die, you're not funny.' That was when I was first starting out, so obviously I took offence and told him to stop being mean.

A year later he messaged me, and then commented again and said, 'Delete your page.' He's been commenting on my stuff for two years now. I've pretty much stopped replying to comments, but in his instance I couldn't resist. I commented back and said, 'When will you give up?' And suddenly he wrote back, 'Sorry, that was my friend.' That must be one really bored friend you have there, buddy.

It's taken a lot of time to toughen up against the online bullies. I used to feel like I had to degrade myself whenever I saw a hurtful comment. Inside, I would agree with the nasty trolls and think, 'Yeah, sorry, I'm not that funny.' Looking back, I have no idea why I did that. Who even are these troll people? I have no idea, especially that kid that has been at it for at least two years of his precious life.

I went to fill up my car the other day, and this dude who has been really vocal about hating me online was the gas attendant. It was the weirdest IRL interaction of my life. He just slowly walked out and filled up my car for me like

everything was totally normal. I have yet to come across someone who has actually told me to my face that I'm not funny.

In real life, I actually get along a lot better with people who don't like my page. One guy that hated me heaps online is now a really good friend. I took him to the hospital the

'I'VE LEARNT THE BEST THING TO DO WITH TROLLS IS FLOAT ABOVE THEIR SASSY SLUDGE.'

other day when he cut his finger. That's just basic troll support right there. Can't have a cut finger while you are typing out mad hate at 2am in Mum's basement. Jokes. Love you, bro.

I actually think both girls and guys get equal amounts of weirdness from trolls online now. I've never felt like I got more creepy crap sent through for being female. Like, it's 2015 — you get weirdness from dogs. I get a few old men saying gross stuff, but that's nowhere near as bad as the naked pictures. I absolutely hate getting sent naked pictures. I don't want to see any of that, no thank you, sir.

I've learnt the best thing to do with trolls is float above their sassy sludge. You shouldn't be able to hear their nasty comments over the sound of applause, laughter and chocolates being showered down upon your awesomeness anyway. If you are getting negative comments online, just ignore it. It's pretty obvious that if someone has to make others feel bad about themselves, they are a dickhead. Screw them.

At the same time, if something is really bothering you — tell people around you. I think it's really important to talk about these things when they happen. Don't let anything bottle up. One day your problems will all bubble over like a Mentos in Coke, and everything around you will get seriously sticky. I never told anyone how I felt when I was bullied and I really should have. Sharing is caring.

Things Jamie can't do with technology

I can't email.
I don't know how to send files on Dropbox.
I don't know how to change my profile picture.
I don't know where my YouTube videos go on my computer
    when I export them.
I don't know what 'The Cloud' is.
I don't know how to resize photos.
I can't forward emails.
I can't cc anyone in emails.
I don't know how to find my analytics.
I don't know how to change my banner.
I don't answer my phone.
I don't answer the home phone.
I don't understand the point of my iPad.
I don't know how to work the radio in my car.
I don't understand radio stations.
I don't know how to use iMessage.
I don't know how to put music on iTunes.
I don't now how to use YouTube.

Not many people know this, but I'm like an old lady in
eighteen-year-old form. I've told you this several times
already in this book, it's time to let the truth shine.

~~~~~~

Apart from the technology, I think I've adapted to online life. My personality in my videos is becoming a lot closer to what I think I'm like in real life. I'm not Jamie with the nerd pants any more, I'm just Jamie in her pyjama pants. Except I'm probably much more inappropriate in real life than I am in my videos. Camera Jamie is just an exaggerated version of me, with a few fun twists. Like I said, my obsession with Channing Tatum isn't actually real — that's just a long-running gag I've held on to. Sorry, Channing. Stop calling me.

If you want to be a YouTuber, I would say go for it. I definitely think it's possible for people to start out now, you just have to be original and be yourself. That's so boring and clichéd, but I think that's the best place to start. Just think, whatever I'm doing, do the opposite. You'll be sweet. Make

'I'M NOT JAMIE WITH THE NERD PANTS ANY MORE, I'M JUST JAMIE IN HER PYJAMA PANTS.'

sure you're having fun. Post stuff that you think is funny, because chances are there is a group out there with the exact same sense of humour as you. But at the same time, don't take it to heart if people don't like your stuff. Not everyone will think you are great or funny or cool or pretty. It's impossible to please everyone in the whole world. Just please yourself.

And, finally, follow your dreams. Except if those dreams are about Dave Franco dying at the hand of an exploding cigar. Then please, please don't.

Some quick online advice

So I clearly don't know anything about being on the Internet or being a human, but that isn't going to stop me from telling you what you should and shouldn't do online. Here are some basic guidelines for success:*

Do

Post whatever you want online (except naked pictures).

If you think you look good in a selfie — post it. Whatever makes you feel good. You go, girlfriend.

Be as positive as you can online, hate is forever.

Don't

Post fully naked photos — do whatever you want in private but trust me, it will end badly.

Don't say anything mean about anyone, especially yourself.

---

* I thought this list would be a lot longer ... all I'm saying is do what you want. But be safe.

Cool
Pants
↪

8

•••••••••••••••••••••••••••

When I Started
Getting
Recognised

'I REMEMBER
THE FIRST
TIME I GOT
RECOGNISED,
IT WAS AT THE
NAPIER A&P
SHOW.'

I REMEMBER THE FIRST TIME I GOT REC-

ognised, it was at the Napier A&P show. In New Zealand, we have these annual farm-type events with rides and sheep everywhere. New Zealand really is exactly how you think it is, by the way. You can't move for sheep. I am, actually, a sheep in a human suit. Anyway, I got recognised. A whole bunch of people got a photo with me, and then that started to happen more and more.

When I had about seven million likes (that's how I measure time now), I went to Auckland and had some Carl's Jr. with my good friend and superstar pop singer Jamie McDell. All of the workers came out and started getting photos with us, and then suddenly I got properly mobbed by people trying to get photos and getting me to sign things.

'I JUST HAD TO SIT
AT THE CONCERT
THE WHOLE NIGHT
LIKE THE POPE,
WAVING DOWN AT
THIS HUGE CROWD
OF PEOPLE.'

I thought to myself, 'I'm never actually going to be able to leave this Carl's Jr.' I'm actually still here, writing this book from under a chair. Send for help, and more fries to table 14.

Another time, at a Justin Bieber concert, security had to get involved and stop people from taking photos. That was when I realised this was ridiculous, that JUSTIN BIEBER was about to get on stage and people would rather focus on a weirdo from Napier. Once one person spots me, it won't stop. I was getting majorly swarmed and my friend had to yank me out of the mob. I was sitting up in the stands after that and everyone down in the crowd noticed me and started waving. I just had to sit at the concert the whole night like the Pope, waving down at this huge crowd of people. Obviously, when Justin came on they were like, 'Okay, bye.'

People around me were mostly fine with the YouTube fame, but I noticed that some people started treating me differently. Sometimes it felt like people just wanted things from me. I just didn't really understand what. A pat on the back? A thumbs up? Especially because I spent some time with no friends, I became super aware of when people were using me. You just get a vibe, you pick up little things.

People make sure they post pictures of you on Instagram, even though nobody actually cares. I know that some people just want to show me off on their arm like a sexy YouTube show pony — but that's crazy. Even those bullies from

Do not be fooled by the shutter shades — that is not Kanye West but in fact me shredding the xylophone.

intermediate have since tried to be friends with ME — the girl they laughed at for wearing a cowboy hat. Who's laughing now, eh?

People would comment online telling me that I suck, but would then get mad when I blocked them and deleted their comments. I bumped into one girl in town, just a few months after she did this exact thing to me online. She acted all sweet and asked for a photo with me. I was shocked, but I don't like conflict so I just smiled through it. Bottling up the pain, exactly what I told you not to do. As I said earlier, rise above it all. I still don't understand what anyone thinks they have to gain from me. The joke's on them if they think I'm worth all the effort, to be honest.

I don't want to keep going on about how much it sucks to be friends with me, but it actually sucks being friends with me now. If you were thinking of trying to be friends with me, run a million miles in the opposite direction. I'm bad news. Your life will suck. My friends asked if they could put a bean bag over my head because my presence is so annoying for them in public. We can't go to malls, the cinema, or any school area around three o'clock. Once I was filming with *20/20* and I told the crew that I needed to be out by 3pm and they didn't believe me. The school bell rang and all the kids just crowded around me. I remember looking at the cameraman with his camera above his head and just thinking, 'I told you so.'

'MY FRIENDS ASKED IF THEY COULD PUT A BEAN BAG OVER MY HEAD BECAUSE MY PRESENCE IS SO ANNOYING FOR THEM IN PUBLIC.'

'I'VE NEVER BEEN SENT ANYTHING TOO WEIRD OR STALKED AT HOME, APART FROM THE TIME A WATERMELON AND A SLEDGEHAMMER TURNED UP.'

My parents were scared of people knowing my last name and figuring out where I lived. They were cautious because they genuinely thought someone was going to kidnap me. But then they just got used to it. And so did I. I've never been sent anything too weird or stalked at home, apart from the time a watermelon and a sledgehammer turned up on our doorstep randomly.

My family have been there from the start, so they've been able to adapt with the channel as it has grown. When they realised it was a possible career path for me, they relaxed into the idea a bit more. 'My daughter makes money off her Internet videos,' they would beam, as other people frowned deeply at my life choices. It sounds worse than it is.

"MY DAUGHTER MAKES MONEY OFF HER INTERNET VIDEOS," THEY WOULD BEAM, AS OTHER PEOPLE FROWNED DEEPLY AT MY LIFE CHOICES.'

Often, the general public are absolute maniacs. They just grab you and pull you every which way like a rag doll. Or they see a crowd around me, and hover until they figure out why I'm famous. When people ask me what I do I just say, 'Oh, I make videos on the Internet' like it's totally normal. Most of the time, people don't care or, if they are old, they don't understand. A middle-aged man came up to me at the mall once and got a photo. Ten minutes later he came back and asked me, 'Who actually are you?' and I just said, 'No-one important.'

I've been mobbed by a crowd once, and this older lady yelled a question at me. 'ARE YOU LORDE?!' she shrieked through the teens. 'No, sorry,' I said. She didn't stick around to find out who this fake Lorde wannabe really was. Hey lady, you missed out. All I'm saying is, they haven't let Lorde write a book yet. Booyah.

'ARE YOU LORDE?!'

DAD'S TAKE
Jamie brings bush-dwelling friends on holiday

'Things have changed a bit for us when we holiday. When we travel as a family now in New Zealand, we often have to call security ahead of visiting places. Some stores can be quite risky, so we take those safety measures just in case. When we went on our family holiday to Brisbane, there were people camped out in the bushes outside our hotel — that was quite scary.'

It's different meeting people at YouTube events — people are more patient and nice because they've put time aside to see you. So thank you, if you've been kind to me out on tour. I love meeting followers at YouTube things, they are so gentle and nice. One girl made me cry, another guy came up to me crying and thanking me for giving him confidence. I started bawling immediately, we were all just crying and hugging a lot.

It's so intense to feel so loved, I will never get used to that emotional side at the YouTube meet and greets. It's so overwhelming. I never cry usually, it's just so weird to have people lining up for hours to meet you. I spend so much time alone in my bedroom making videos, it's easy to forget about the people watching at the other end. So I just hug and cry and cry some more. And then of course suck it up and forget it ever happened.

Often people think I'm stuck up or rude when they first meet me, but I'm really just painfully awkward. To people approaching me in real life: please don't yell, and be very, very quiet. Approach me like a lion that's about to pounce and kill you. Steadily, slowly. Maybe that's too violent, maybe a tiger. No, a leopard. You never know what leopards are going to do. I won't kill you though, I promise. Just be cool and don't flip your lid. Okay?

Often people want to touch me, and caress my hair. This is a huge no-no. It's important for people to remember that we are actually just people like you. You can't just pat us randomly. We're still human beings that get weirded out by strangers stroking them. One girl asked to smell me once, and then got mad at me because I didn't smell like anything. She was so disappointed. I'm sorry to let you down if you are reading this, smelling lady. Please enjoy this Jamie scratch-and-sniff panel:

Scratch 'n' Sniff
JAMIE'S WORLD

Jokes, still smells like nothing lol.

'IT'S IMPORTANT
FOR PEOPLE TO
REMEMBER THAT
WE ARE ACTUALLY
JUST PEOPLE LIKE
YOU. YOU CAN'T
JUST PAT US
RANDOMLY.'

John Lennon ain't dead

Is this a normal thing for legs to do?

International sloth

Travel tips

Touring around and meeting you guys, I've picked up a few handy travel tips. Want me to share? You don't get a choice! You're the reader and I'm the writer! Why am I so angry? Not sure.

Bring water

In almost any travel situation, the chance for dehydration is very high. If you are flying, the sky sucks out all the moisture in your body to use for rain. I'm pretty sure that's how that works. Next time it rains, spare a thought for all the dry people in the plane above you.

Bring a backpack with more water

Something I found out in Thailand: nothing will prepare you for the amount of sweat that will leave your body faster than you can say 'Is there air-conditioning in here?'

Bring a spare T-shirt

If you're in South-East Asia, that is; you'll inevitably sweat through the first one.

Be a plane zombie

The night before a long-haul flight, try to stay up as late as possible. This means that when you get on the plane, you'll be so exhausted that you will go out like a light. Unless of course you don't, and instead get a taste for human flesh.

Always have a jacket on hand

Even though you are closer to the sun, do not be fooled — planes are always colder than you imagine they are going to be. Don't be fooled.

Headphones and hair ties

Two essential items that go missing so often when travelling. Where do they get sucked away to? Somewhere out there must be the biggest knotted ball of hair ties and headphones. One day it will roll through the city and trample us all.

Get a donut

It's a healthy tradition of mine to always get donuts when I'm at the airport. One jelly and one glazed. The Jamie Special.

Find the sockets

Another useful thing to do at airports when you have time to kill is to walk around and see where all of the power sockets are. That way, the next time you are back there on your adventures, you'll know exactly where to head to charge up your phone or laptop. Useful, I know.

Talk to people

This is a spooky tip for the more socially challenged, but I find airports a really freeing place to practise chatting to people. First of all, everyone's bored and just killing time. Second of all, you can just make stuff up about yourself because you are never going to see these people again.

Halfway through these conversations people often say, 'Do I know you from somewhere?' and I just lie to their face. I tell them that I'm on a gap year, or I'm in a drug cartel. Kidding, don't do that last one — you will get arrested.

9

••••••••••••••••••••

Don't Press This Leopard's Panic Button

'EVEN AT SCHOOL I COULDN'T SIT IN ASSEMBLY WITH EVERYONE ELSE, I HAD TO SIT SEPARATELY. LIKE A LITTLE NERVOUS QUEEN.'

A BIG THING THAT YOU PROBABLY DON'T GET

to see in my videos is that I have a really anxious side. I had a panic attack once. I don't like being in crowds, even at school I couldn't sit in assembly with everyone else, I had to sit separately. Like a little nervous Queen. Even at church I often have to leave if there are too many people. This feeling can sometimes get tough when I am faced with huge crowds all waiting and watching me.

For example, at one YouTube meet and greet I started freaking out at everyone pushing through the door. I had to leave almost straight away to have a chill-out away from all the chaos. I felt really bad about that because I missed about 60 people who had come to see me, but I was honestly having a full-blown meltdown.

Being awkward on stage at vidcon

Despite what my videos might suggest, I am definitely an introvert. It happened as I started to get a bit older. Every year, I withdrew a bit more and became more of an outsider. Now, I'm more straight up about it — I just plain don't like talking to people. I especially hate group conversations, I just won't talk. I refuse. If there are more than three people in the room, I'll let anyone else talk but me. Even with my own friends. Even with my mum. I just always end up saying the wrong thing at the wrong time. Talking is such a pain, right? I can't be the only person that feels this way? Or maybe I am …

My mum has always said that I had a very good sense of humour from a young age. But I've never been one of those performer-y types who likes standing up in a group and having all the attention on them. I don't want all eyes on me, I'd much rather they be on someone else. So I don't know actually where this Jamie's World stuff came from, it's all very weird. Now that I have all this attention, it truly sucks, to be honest. I don't know why I do it. Every day is agony.

When I get up on stage I get really anxious, I don't like having lots of people surrounding me and looking at me.

'I DON'T WANT ALL EYES ON ME, I'D MUCH RATHER THEY BE ON SOMEONE ELSE. SO I DON'T KNOW ACTUALLY WHERE THIS JAMIE'S WORLD STUFF CAME FROM.'

When I know the spotlight is on me, I get really dizzy. One time I didn't want to face the big crowd, and I was actually hyperventilating on the side of the stage. But, because I'm a huge pro, I had to put on my Jamie face and get out there. The second I turned to leave the stage, my face went totally white as I ran off.

People tell me I'm fine on stage but I don't believe it. There's a trend for YouTubers to do tours and live shows, but I'll stick to the bedroom for now. I spend so much time being goofy, and still struggle to be normal in front of big groups IRL. But then, I think it's normal to have ten million people watching me online. It makes no sense. I much prefer talking to a camera than a room of people. You know when people say 'Just pretend everyone's naked'? I just pretend that every person is a camera.

'I SPEND SO
MUCH TIME
BEING GOOFY,
AND STILL
STRUGGLE TO
BE NORMAL IN
FRONT OF BIG
GROUPS IRL.'

My biggest, baddest fears

I have just told you about my fear of crowds, which is a little more rational than the other things that keep me up at night. I actually encounter crowds in my daily life, unlike most of the things on this list. I've never been afraid of the dark, or ghosts or any of those old-school scares.

Once I think I had a supernatural encounter in Thailand, but it wasn't that scary. I was walking through a temple alone and I felt a wire at my ankle trip me up. I looked back and there was nothing in the way. We will never know if that was a cheeky ghost or if I am just generally clumsy, but I'm sure you can draw your own conclusions. On with the list.

Zombies

I hate zombies. I've had so many nightmares about zombies storming my house at night, walking all the way to Napier to feast on me. On my twelfth birthday I watched a zombie movie and I've never forgotten it. I mean, I've obviously forgotten what it's called, but the fact that everyone died at the end stuck with me. There's just no way out if zombies are around, and I hate that.

Sharks

I couldn't be in a swimming pool by myself when I was a kid

because I thought a shark would be there. I used to have an irrational fear that a shark would eat me in my bed through the carpet. All very normal and healthy fears.

Pinocchio

His horrible pointy little nose really freaks me out. There's a scary live-action version with Jonathan Taylor Thomas as Pinocchio, which scared me to death. After I saw it I moved my wooden doll out of my room and into my sister's room. She can deal with that wooden lying creep, thank you very much.

Heights

Whenever I'm up high, I'll just freeze and have zero balance. I once tried to walk around the outside of Auckland's Sky Tower with Cody Simpson (whatever, no big deal). I just froze up completely and couldn't take any more steps. Cody Simpson held his hand out to me and I still couldn't do it. And that's Cody flippin' Simpson!

Chickens

Once my mum left all the doors open because she was drying the floors after cleaning them. She had to go out somewhere so I was by myself, scared and alone. In my vulnerable state, all these local chickens chose to menacingly surround the house. I looked from left to right and there were chickens everywhere. I had to lock myself in the office and call my neighbour to scare them away. I just don't like how they stare, and I don't like how they think.

Here's me at my birthday party with a light sabre. I knighted everyone at the party with it.

My first Jamie's World cover photo. You can't see, but I'm in my pyjama pants. Setting the standard.

My first million. I'm clearly very happy about it and thank goodness I dressed up for the occasion.

1 Million

I think this is my first ever selfie. Kim Kardashian could learn a thing or two from me.

We had an Art Deco dress-up day in Year 13. I'm adding my own flair with the socks and sandals, but it's also because I hate showing my feet to people.

Here's me and my braces at my first radio interview. I had to get up really early before school for this. I was at about 795k on Facebook.

This is the original Jamie's World Facebook profile picture. Also where I did my first comments burn — someone commented, 'Oh my God' and I commented back, 'People call me Jamie, not God.' Still real proud of that one.

Here's me reaching out for my goals and not quite getting there.

I made a meme about accidentally using salt instead of sugar. To make it really authentic, I actually used salt. It was disgusting, but I think shows my commitment to the cause.

This is the first time ever someone asked for a photo with me in public, and about the last time I could go out casually to local events.

Before our high school graduation dinner. I had to dry my hair out the window on the way there like a dog. Great for that tousled look.

A very natural Jamie's World photo. Not many people know this, but I set th whole thing up and tried to make it loo super casual. Not bad, right?

This is at my first ball, lying down. What else would I be doing? I couldn't breathe in my dress and my feet hurt.

At my second ball, having a sleep again.

Ten million likes!

Here's me in nerd character on our athletics day. That's my WHOLE SCHOOL, by the way.

'YOU KNOW WHEN PEOPLE SAY, "JUST PRETEND EVERYONE'S NAKED"? I JUST PRETEND THAT EVERY PERSON IS A CAMERA.'

A Jamie Curry origional↰
ur welcome ⤸
            are they spelt right?

10

•••••••••••••••••••••••••••••••••

I'm So OCD
— No, Like,
Literally

'WELCOME TO REALITY, AND PLEASE FLICK THE LIGHT SWITCH ON AND OFF 37 TIMES BEFORE YOU COME ANY CLOSER.'

IT'S TIME FOR SOME REAL TALK. I HAVE OCD.

I've been to a counsellor to help me deal with it and everything. Turns out that it is somehow linked to the way I get panicky in crowds. You thought this book was going to be all kooky jokes, didn't you? All funny lists and hilarious pictures? Welcome to reality, and please flick the light switch on and off 37 times before you come any closer.

I always used to analyse rooms, that's one of the ways that you can tell if you have OCD. Apparently, if you walk into a room and can close your eyes and recall everything in the room — you're probably a little OCD. People annoy me when they say they're OCD just because they like brushing their teeth the normal amount, or they like using hand sanitiser sometimes. That's not OCD. I'll show you OCD.

If you've seen my videos, you would have noticed that my room looks a little bit like a hotel room. It's almost empty. This is because I can't handle clutter, and it makes me incredibly anxious when things are messy. When I got home from the Amplify tour, I left almost straight away to somewhere else and I didn't have time to unpack. When I finally got home after that, my room was such a mess that I had heart palpitations.

What else? I can't handle dirt or mud or anything like that. I used to have to shut all the doors in the house before bed and line up my slippers perfectly, exactly the same every night. My bed always has to be made perfectly, otherwise I can't sleep. There's only one couch in our family lounge that I can sit on for long periods of time. I can't sit on the same couch that someone else has just sat on. And definitely not in my pyjamas. Those are my sleeping clothes, the most sacred clothes of all.

I like towels and bathmats to be perfectly flat or I can't use them or be near them. I used to have to have both feet on the carpet outside my bathroom when I turned lights off, rather than on the tiles. So I'd have to lean around the door to switch off the light before bed. I'm getting better at it now. I can turn the light off with my feet on the tiles. But I'm still not happy about it.

I also really hate feet. Feet of all kinds, including my own. I never want people to see my feet, I never want to see my

'I CAN'T SIT ON THE SAME COUCH THAT SOMEONE ELSE HAS JUST SAT ON. AND DEFINITELY NOT IN MY PYJAMAS. THOSE ARE MY SLEEPING CLOTHES, THE MOST SACRED CLOTHES OF ALL.'

own feet. I have special socks that I wear every night. It's weird though because I really like hands, that's actually the first thing I notice about a person when I meet them. Hi, I'm Jamie, I hate feet but love hands — could you please straighten out that mat for me before I cry?

I'm really into cleaning things that I use every day. I clean my sneakers every time I wear them. I'm also very fussy about keeping my phone clean. I have this whole system down pat for the best clean. Put a towel down and rest your phone on it. Lightly dribble water on it and gently towel it off. Once a week, treat your phone to a really good baby wipe. It's like a pampering spa for your phone, sort of. A really cheap, obsessive and stressful type of spa.

My life in numbers

It's easy to get bogged down in numbers when you are a YouTuber. I'm not counting views or watching subscriber counts, but I thought it would be fun to run the numbers on my life so far and see what the Jamie calculator spits out. Here are the very scientific totals for me:

5 the number of black jeans I currently own

4 pairs of black leather boots in my wardrobe

3 ChapSticks on hand at all times

71 ChapSticks lost in my life

3 countries I have visited so far

1.72 metres tall

3 broken bones on my clumsy body

5 scars over the years of stupid injury

2 pillows must be under my sleeping head at all times

8 different duvet covers have been on my bed in my life

5500 nice people I've met in real life because of YouTube

1 cowboy hat is too many cowboy hats

40 wheels on my various transport options from unicycle to finger skateboard

23 times I have stubbed my toe on the couch

14,000 kilometres I have driven in the past six months

332 times I have eaten bacon and eggs

4 times I have been mistaken for Lorde

4621 noodles I have eaten

4.30 minutes is my ideal YouTube video length

4,471,000 is the population of New Zealand

5 foods in the world that I am okay with eating

978,000 foods I will visibly gag at the thought of

15,888 Snapchats I have sent

1.7 million likes, the most likes on one of my Facebook photos

3 years of Jamie's World so far

57,000 people in my hometown of Napier

60 cm of long luscious locks

6,743,122 people have asked me if I like curry

21 times a week I have to wash my phone

34 hats I've owned in my short life

5 glasses of water a day is my hydration goal

640 crime show episodes watched by me

1703 songs in my iTunes playlist

105 plays of 'Heart Out' by The 1975 (my most played song)

148 pairs of socks in my life, I do love me some nice socks

'HI, I'M JAMIE, I HATE FEET BUT LOVE HANDS – COULD YOU PLEASE STRAIGHTEN OUT THAT MAT FOR ME BEFORE I CRY?'

This is me in 25years

11

••••••••••••••••••••

This is a Job!
Wait, What?

'I WANT TO MAKE
SOMETHING CLEAR:
I WILL NEVER
HOLD A THING OF
TOOTHPASTE AND
TALK ABOUT HOW
GOOD IT IS FOR FIVE
MINUTES. EVEN FOR
$5 MILLION.'

I'M LUCKY ENOUGH TO SAY THAT YOUTUBE

is now my full-time job, and I hope to build a career around it. YouTube became a job for me once I got my agents on board, and I realised that it could be a source of major, rapper-style dollar bills. I'm kidding.

I still don't actually treat it as a proper *job* job. I'm not crazy about having to make heaps of money all the time or anything, but I also don't think that people should get angry at us for wanting to make a living. There was a crazy hashtag a while back of #YouTubehonestyhour, where followers really lashed out at YouTubers for having sponsored videos.

I want to make something clear: I will never hold a thing of toothpaste and talk about how good it is for five minutes. Even for $5 million. People get angry when they find out

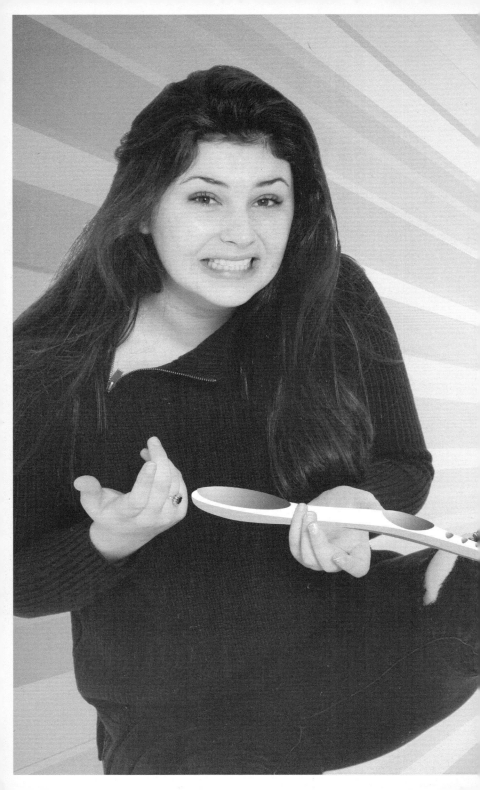

FOR A SUPER-CHEESY SMILE!

JAMIE TOOTHPASTE

NINE OUT OF TEN DENTISTS RECOMMEND 'JAMIE' BRAND TOOTHPASTE.

IT'S CHEESE-FLAVOURED TOO!

we are making money off videos, but I'm like, what else am I supposed to do?! I don't have a job because I'm flying around meeting you guys all the time. One time a girl commented on one of my travel videos saying, 'Good to see our taxes have gone towards your holiday.' That just plain doesn't make sense, sorry, love. The New Zealand Government is not funding my nonsense.

I just want everyone to know that my channel is a job and I do get money for it, but it's never just been about that for me. I've worked very hard for this, even harder than when I won Sportsgirl of the Year twice in a row (thank you very

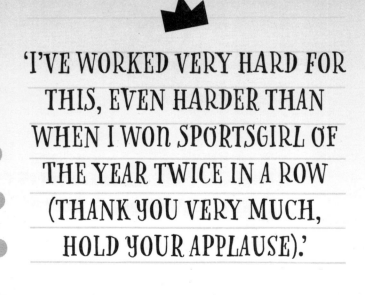

'I'VE WORKED VERY HARD FOR THIS, EVEN HARDER THAN WHEN I WON SPORTSGIRL OF THE YEAR TWICE IN A ROW (THANK YOU VERY MUCH, HOLD YOUR APPLAUSE).'

'THEY GAVE ME THE JOB OF PRINTING OUT RECEIPTS. I PRINTED OUT ABOUT 1000 BY ACCIDENT.'

much, hold your applause). I was preparing all through my last year of high school for this career — teachers never understood that though. I would often fly to Sydney for meetings on the weekend, and fly back on Monday morning to go straight to school and fall asleep under a desk at the back of the classroom. Not a great way to get A's, but a great way to get Z's.

I didn't have a back-up plan when I left school. I didn't know what else I wanted to do. I liked school but I didn't excel at any subjects in particular. I did some work experience and I really hated it. It was still during high school, and I was sick for two of the three days (there's them note skills coming in handy). We had to work at an appliance store. I got there on the last day, and they gave me the job of printing out receipts. I printed out about 1000 by accident.

'SO YOUTUBE IS THE PERFECT (AND ONLY) JOB LEFT FOR ME IN THE WORLD TO DO. I DON'T HAVE TO TALK TO ANYONE, I DON'T HAVE TO GET CHANGED OUT OF MY PYJAMAS.'

The boss got angry so they gave me an even easier job of sticking stickers on dishwashers. I stuck them on wrong.

Not only did I suck at that job, but I hated everything about it. I hated having to wear a work uniform. I hated talking to people I didn't know. I hated having to stick stickers on in a certain way. So YouTube is the perfect (and only) job left for me in the world to do. I don't have to talk to anyone, I don't have to get changed out of my pyjamas. So I'm very lucky, but I'd also be screwed without it. Without YouTube, I'd just be a crazy woman yelling to a wall in her bedroom.

So what comes next after YouTube? Who knows, it's not like there's a big blueprint for online celebrities. We are all just figuring it out as we go along, and I'm going to try to get as far as I can up the career ladder without taking my pyjamas off. It is a goal of mine to get into acting, so I'm hoping that YouTube can be a good platform for that. Directors are looking to the Internet for roles more and more now. I just hope they don't unlock all those private videos of me mouth-breathing.

Who would I like to meet in the future?

Grace Helbig (YouTuber)

I really want to meet Grace Helbig because she's such a funny YouTuber. I think we have a strong resemblance in our total weirdness. Not that I'm copying her at all, but I just like that she's awkward like me. Grace just plays it off a lot better than I do. I think we'd get along really well. A girl can dream.

The Queen (Queen)

It would be cool to meet the Queen, but I'm also a bit scared that she would be boring to talk to. What would we even talk about? Would I have to eat an asparagus sandwich? I've changed my mind. And you have to bow and curtsy and all that stuff. Screw that. I wouldn't even be allowed to tell her 'Yaaaasss, Queen', I bet.

Angelina Jolie (Actress)

I really like Angelina Jolie, she's just so effortlessly cool all the time. She's basically the exact opposite of me, so I think that the universe would explode if we were in the same room. She's very good at acting, and just seems like a really good person. I feel like she would get me a cup of tea if I went over to her house, even though I don't like tea. I'd be polite and take it. Also *Sandra Bullock*. She and Ange can come over for scones.

~~~~~~

I always want to use my YouTube channel, but I don't want it to rule my life. I'll hopefully stick to the once-a-week (or once a month ...) and that will be me. All going well, my channel will follow my life as a successful actor. And then I'll have a band of minions filming me on sets and things. Hopefully. Or I'll just tie a GoPro to my big head as I walk around doing nothing and eating curly fries. Either way, you guys can be there for the ride. I'll always have Twitter and social media to stay connected, but I don't see myself on YouTube forever. Or maybe I'll just live and die on Jamie's World. Stay tuned.

DAD'S TAKE
Jamie makes Internet hay

'I've always said to Jamie, "Make hay while the sun shines."
YouTube has certainly opened doors for her and I hope that
it can be a springboard into her next major venture. She's
ready to start flying now. We've put a lot of effort and love
into her, and I think she's ready.'

Going to LA for VidCon has meant I can scope out the
Hollywood scene. I'm hoping to make friends there because
I really need someone to live with. And I don't know how to
live by myself. LA people, get in touch. Paris Hilton, I know
you are reading this. You've got to have a room free, right?
Cate Blanchett? We shared a few happy moments together
at the *Cinderella* premiere one time? Dave Franco? I don't
want to sound threatening but don't make me have another
dream about you ...

If I make it to America, I want to take the Sandra Bullock
path. She can act funny but also do serious really well.
I'd want to transition into serious stuff eventually in my
fantasy acting career that I'm making up in my head right
now. I also think I look a bit like Sandra Bullock — hopefully
at the very least I could be her body double or something.
I'm prepared to go to fake space for you, Sandy, just give me

a job. And a room. And tell me how to work the washing machine. That's all.

My favourite movies

I want to get into acting, but it's hard for me to see a lot of films because the only movies I go to now are premieres. That sounds snobby and terrible, but I can't go to young people hubs like 'the movies'. Partially because I'll get mobbed, but mostly because I'm an old lady and I say things like 'young people hubs'. My favourite movies aren't the usual classics you see in these types of lists.

For example, I haven't seen a single *Star Wars* film. But that didn't stop me from collecting light sabres. I know, cool, right? I had three of them, which is three more than any person should have. In case you were wondering, there is a way to be geekier than a *Star Wars* fan — just be an exclusive die-hard light sabre fan. You're welcome.

Anyway, here are a few of my favourites right now:

The Great Gatsby

I absolutely love the 1920s era — I find it really fascinating and beautiful to look at. I think that old Leo D was much better looking when he was younger, though. There's

Jamie's two cents, Leo, burn. I hope he doesn't read this! Jamie, don't be stupid, of course he's not going to read this. Leo, if you're reading this, I'm sorry.

The Perks of Being a Wallflower

Look at me, a walking, talking teenage cliché. This is a movie about an introverted kid getting taken in and shown the ropes by two crazy cool senior students. I think it's pretty much every weird kid's dream.

The Runaways

This is me being alternative and hip. Did you know I have rips in my jeans as I write this? Really, it's a surprise that I like this grungy rocker film. But this is a very cool movie. It's based on the lives of Joan Jett's original kickass girl group The Runaways. The fashion is amazing, and I really like how the women don't need anything in their lives. They just like to cruise around and be a little bit mental. The dream.

The Rum Diary

This movie stars Johnny Depp and Amber Heard. It's about a writer — you could probably tell that already because it's got 'diary' in the title. Kind of like how my book has 'book' in the title. I like it when things are kept simple. Johnny Depp plays Hunter S Thompson, who was this wacko writer in the '70s. He drives the coolest car and has such extreme fashion.

Why do
I always look
in pain ahaha

12

••••••••••••••••••••

How Do I Adult?

'I'M ONLY SURE
OF ONE THING:
I DON'T KNOW
HOW TO ADULT,
BUT I KNOW
THAT IT SEEMS
TO SUCK A LOT.'

ALL THIS TALK OF THE FUTURE LEADS US TO

a terrible, terrible truth: I'm getting older. We are all getting older. You are older than when you first opened this book. I have taken that time from you, sucked it right out of you like a youth vampire. As I leave my tomato-sauce-bandit teenage years, I'm only sure of one thing: I don't know how to adult, but I know that it seems to suck a lot. To me, it's terrifying and full of things I either don't know how to do, or don't like doing at all.

To be honest, I'm just not sure I know how to survive on my own without someone making sure I don't hurt myself, burn the house down or eat something toxic. I tried to do the desert island thing to see if I could figure out how to keep myself alive without my mum or the Internet. It didn't go very well.

'I'M JUST NOT SURE
I KNOW HOW TO
SURVIVE ON MY
OWN WITHOUT
SOMEONE MAKING
SURE I DON'T HURT
MYSELF, BURN THE
HOUSE DOWN OR EAT
SOMETHING TOXIC.'

Three things on my desert island

I'm going to be the annoying person that says water, food and a house. That's too boring, isn't it? I'm so sorry, I really thought I would have come up with something better, too. Like life, this book has highs and lows, fun surprises and totally predictable answers. I'll think harder, surely I've got a better idea somewhere in the ol' brainbox.

Okay, I'd take a group of my closest friends. Is there going to be fresh water on the island? Hmm, probably not. Let's say I can evaporate the seawater like Bear Grylls and drink from that, so I don't need to cart water along. I'd bring cooking utensils and a comfy sleeping bag. Oh but what about food? Is there a Denny's?? Ergh, guess I'd have to learn to eat fish and make some sort of fruity science lab from nature. Let's not go to the island, please. I need to have curly fries.

What do adults actually do? An undercover investigation

I've been spending more and more time with this alien adult life form recently, and I've been doing a bit of low-key research on this scary species. They don't know I'm not one of them, I've been wearing a pantsuit and talking about drapes. Here's a list of fancy adult habits that I have secretly observed, and secretly need to learn how to do:

Drink coffee

I hate coffee, and I hate how much adults drink coffee. Whenever I'm around them, I will stretch to a hot chocolate just to fit in. I don't even like hot chocolate very much, but I still put on a brave face and hold my little paper cup like the biggest hot-drink-swilling grown-up in town. Maybe I'm the problem? It's weird that I don't even like hot chocolate, right? It makes my gums feel weird. Oh man, I am the weirdest human being with the weirdest problems.

I don't know how coffee works, or even how to make it. When people come over to my house, I ask them if they would like a cup of coffee. If they say yes, I tell them that I was being polite and there's no way I know how to make their special sophisticated potion. I thought you put the beans straight into the water and they dissolved and made coffee. Never come to my house.

Drinking wine

This is another thing, just like coffee, where I think someone must be lying somewhere along the line here. Wine tastes disgusting, fact. The other day I had a freak-out at the supermarket and bought a $70 champagne for no reason. I couldn't drink it! And that's fancy champagne like the Queen would drink!

Eating oysters

Who are all these adults who pretend to like oysters? What is an oyster? Who was the first person to eat that thing? Did they do it as a dare? The only things I know about oysters are that you need a little knife thing to open it, and they are very expensive. I imagine it tastes like what a fish smells like. There are still barnacles all over them, not even cleaned or anything. I just don't understand, but also I have a strict 'nothing from the sea' eating policy.

Sharing food

I've recently been made aware of this horrific trend to order huge plates of food for the table and pick little bits off yourself. This is my nightmare. First of all, my palate is so specific that I often can't stomach anything on a tapas menu. Secondly, germ alert! Keep your soiled fingers and forks to yourself, please, I'll just eat this vat of curly fries that I brought from home.

Wearing boring clothes

I don't know how to dress like an adult. I don't even dress appropriately now. I'm always in ripped jeans and turtlenecks and stuff. I always look ridiculous, I just wear whatever makes me feel hilarious. When you get older you have to wear much more reserved clothing. You aren't allowed ripped jeans, which is a pain because I buy jeans FOR the rips. I also think it's frowned upon for adults to wear ponchos, which sucks because I just bought one that I was keen to try out.

Eating fancy food

To paint you a picture of my ideal dinner date: my favourite restaurants are the types that have kids' colouring books lying around, where your food is delivered to you in a cardboard race car. I don't eat at fancy dinner places. Recently, we went to a famous Auckland restaurant, run by a very famous New Zealand chef called Al Brown. He's like our Gordon Ramsay, just with less swearing and more glasses. But at the time, I had no idea who he was. I'm still as oblivious as an eight-year-old staring at a cardboard box.

The waiter came over, and everyone at our table placed their fancy orders. I asked for the poutine (fries with cheese curd and gravy) without any of the cheese curd or the gravy. Just fries basically, I basically wanted McDonald's-quality fries. The waiter walked away and somebody kicked me hard under the table. The man who had taken our order was Al Brown himself. I just ordered fries off Al Brown. That's like asking Coco Chanel if she would like to go shopping at KMart. Oh well.

Cushions

Adults love talking about cushions and home decor like their life depends on it. I always hear them in department stores saying things like 'That cushion looks so good, I love that cushion, I need those cushions.' I don't care about cushions. I don't care about rugs. When does this start to happen?! I'm scared of the day I wake up and want to buy a rug. I hope it's not too soon.

No sick days

You can't wake up in the morning and be sick and not go to school. Sometimes I have to catch a plane somewhere for work and I wake up and just want Mum to write a note to excuse me. I'd always get Mum to write notes at school and say I'm not feeling well. As an adult, if you miss deadlines and stuff, there's no Mum pass any more. There's no get-out-of-jail-free card. You have to just suck it up, and take all your rage out on all your new plush pillows.

Birthdays are bad

You don't get a day off for your birthday as an adult. When you get older, your birthday isn't an excuse to get away with stuff any more. You can't demand stuff just because it's your birthday. Birthdays are exciting as a kid, but seem to be really sad as an adult. I'll be thirty soon, divorced and alone drinking gross wine and horrible dissolved coffee beans on my birthday. At least my huge expensive rug will mop up my tears.

Organising the dentist

When you are an adult you have to remember to take yourself to the dentist, which sucks. I don't know how to do that. I wouldn't know what number to call, I don't know my dentist's name or even my doctor. I need special attention as well because two of my front teeth aren't real teeth. That's right, a Jamie's World exclusive: I have two false teeth. They slowly erode away, which is gross, so I have to get them 'topped up'. Without Mum to organise this, you can look forward to me looking a lot more hillbilly very soon.

Doing dishes

I don't actually know how to use a dishwasher. This sounds

really terrible, doesn't it? I think that dishes are probably very simple to do. When my mum goes away, she leaves a note that says 'Jamie, just press the big button.' I still found a way to mess that up. Let's just say that I have learnt that you don't use the squirty soap in the dishwasher under any circumstances, unless you are looking to have a solo foam party.

Paying bills and rent

I don't know how to find a house to live in. I just don't know what to look for. How do you know if there are ghosts or leaks or weird neighbours or wasp nests? I also didn't know that you have to pay for water and electricity on top of everything else. How does any adult afford this life? Does the water get counted by the cup? I'm just going to collect rainwater like Bear Grylls and pocket major cash. I hope I can figure out where to pay all these bills by the time I'm living alone. I can definitely see myself living in darkness with only candles for light and warmth, just because I did my bills all wrong.

Washing clothes

I know for clothes you need to do a cold wash and warm wash, but I don't know which temperature works for what.

Every time I do a wash my clothes come out like dolls' clothes, which is cute for a few seconds until I realise I have nothing left to wear. I don't need my jeans to shrink any more, I'm having a hard enough time fitting them as it is. I'm also not sure how to dry clothes properly; even as I write this I'm sitting in the sun so that my damp just-washed sweater can dry off. Yep. The sad, cold, wet truth.

Cooking

A big thing I don't know a lot about in adult life is cooking. I never know what temperature to put the oven on, and I'm constantly worried about either burning my food or undercooking it and contracting a deadly virus. Cooking is a mystery to me, and I'm impatient so I end up turning up the heat and charring the outside of things whilst the inside stays frozen solid. Bookings are open for my restaurant now, by the way. The one thing I need to take a class in is making spaghetti bolognese. Is there a spag bol night class out there? Or is that too specific? I just think that's all I need to get by in this life. Nutritionists might say otherwise, but this isn't their book.

COOKING

with

JAMIE

(Curry, not Oliver. And Curry my name, not curry the dish. Never mind, here are my favourite recipes)

I'm nervous about cooking as an adult, but that doesn't mean I don't have a few killer recipes already under my belt. Here's a warning for all chefs, clean eaters, raw eaters, vegans, paleo, sugar-free, health-conscious readers out there: just rip this section out and throw it straight in the nearest fire.

JAMIE'S SOMETIMES-PANCAKE SCONES

You'll need:

About two cups of flour
Maybe 50 grams-ish of butter
Big amount of milk

To serve:

Raspberry jam (no other type of jam is
acceptable in my kitchen)
Freshly whipped cream
(cream in a can is the devil's work)

1 Preheat the oven to bake at 220°C, or something
   vaguely close to that. Have a fiddle around, have an
   experiment. Just see what works for you. Baking is
   as much an exact science as it is personal expression
   (please note: baking is 100% an exact science).
2 Chuck your two cups of flour in a bowl. Should you sift
   it? Let fate decide. Lumps give character, lumps are
   what makes us human.
3 Using the little bit of butter, get your hands right in
   there and use it to make big buttery breadcrumb-
   looking things in the flour. Does this make sense at all?
   Does this sound right? Basically you are giving the flour
   a big old massage with the butter. That sounds gross,
   and it is gross.
4 Add in the milk and mix it all around like you just don't

care. Use a wooden spoon, a ruler or a badminton racquet.

5 When you think you've added enough milk — add more milk. It will look like a risky move but just roll with it. If it goes too far you'll just end up with awesome scone-pancakes, and who doesn't want two of the greatest food groups coming together like that in a beautiful accident?

6 Plop the mixture onto your baking tray in small squares. I guess put some non-stick stuff down before that. Damn, I should have said that first. Sorry, start again.

7 Get some MORE MILK.

8 Using a rubber spatula or a hairbrush, dip into the milk and smooth it over the scone piles to give it a milky glaze. This smooths it out and seals in the moisture. Look at that! An actual pro tip!

9 Bake them for 15 minutes in the oven, and during this time locate the raspberry jam (scoop it onto the most vintage Pinterest plate you can find).

10 Whip up the cream until it is as fluffy and smooth as the hair of an angel.

11 When the scones have cooled, chop 'em in half and dollop on the delicious.

JAMIE'S NEATO BURRITO

You'll need:

Large onion

Mince

Burrito flavour sachet

Lettuce

Tomato

Carrot

Cheese

To serve:

Tortilla

Corn chips

1 Cut up the onion into tiny bits. Cry your heart out. Cry for every mean comment, every person who has ever wronged you, every emotional performance you've seen on *Britain's Got Talent*. Get it all out, the onion is your excuse.

2 Get your mince and mash it up until it is as fine as sand. It's no surprise that I really don't like mince in its normal form, so I have to make it edible by pulping it up. You don't have to do this but I'll judge you silently if you don't.

3 Chuck the mince and onion in a pan, and cook it until it starts sticking to the bottom. I don't know if this is a scientifically proven method — you can also just look to see when it starts to go brown.

4 Mix in burrito flavour sachet with a cup of water. Do not try to drink this as an exciting beverage, things will not end well for you.
5 Cut up heaps of lettuce, heaps of tomato, a little bit of carrot and a little bit of cheese.
6 Here you have two options, because I am a diverse cook. The first is to wrap it all up into a burrito, the second is to pile it on top of corn chips for nachos. That's two dinners sorted for you right there.

JAMIE'S HEALTH-PACKED VERY EASY WAFFLES

You'll need:

One egg (chicken's)

Cup of flour

¾ cup of milk

50 grams melted butter

(made this one up, but seems right)

To serve:

Maple syrup

Banana

1 Mix all the ingredients together in a bowl. This is so easy, even I can do it with only minimal spillage and minor injury.

2 Put the mixture into the waffle maker. Oh yeah, so you need a waffle maker to do this. Got to this step and don't have a waffle maker? Rejig the mixture and make some more cool scones or something. Make cupcakes. Make a smoothie. Make paste. Make it up as you go along.

3 Should produce three waffles (it's fine to eat three waffles).

4 Drown in maple syrup.

5 Decorate with cut-up banana. (SEE? FRUIT! HEALTH-PACKED!)

JAMIE'S PERFECTLY TIMED SPAGHETTI ON TOAST

You'll need:

White bread

Tinned spaghetti

Loads of butter

1 Put the toast in the toaster and watch it until it's starting to brown slightly. Don't stay too close to the toaster or it will burn your eyelashes off.

2 When you see your toast toasting, dash over to the microwave and put in your spaghetti for 1½ minutes. Make sure you cover the bowl, you don't want it to look like a tomato got murdered on your time.

3 This is where the precision timing really comes into play. When there's 40 seconds left on your spaghetti, get that toast out of that toaster ASAP. Not a second to waste at this stage if you want perfection.

4 You have 40 seconds left to butter that toast within an inch of its life — use every second as if it were your last.

5 Pour the spaghetti onto the deliciously soggy butter toast.

6 Enjoy your perfectly timed, perfectly processed meal.

(I have an alternative version where I replace spaghetti with a poached egg. Intrigued? Read on.)

JAMIE'S BEAUTIFUL-ON-THE-INSIDE POACHED EGG

You'll need:

Egg

Water

Vinegar

More confidence than you've ever mustered before

1 Boil water in a pot until it's slightly bubbling.
2 Crack an egg into a little bowl to let it know what a cool shape to be is.
3 Pour a splash of vinegar into the water, and swirl it around into an exciting hot whirlpool.
4 Pour in the egg using a constant and confident flow. This is easily the worst part, don't doubt yourself and be strong.
5 Stare down at the terrible mess you've made and wonder how that is ever going to turn into an edible thing.
6 Take a big guess as to when you think the inside is cooked to how you like it. I normally run a few laps of the kitchen and do some push-ups and it's all done by then. They say it's good to eat eggs after working out, see I know stuff?!
7 Eat your hideous creation.

Dream dinner guests

All this talk of food has made me hungry, so I thought I'd sit down and have a deep hard think about who I would invite to my lavish dinner party of milky scones, ugly poached eggs and perfectly timed spaghetti. That's another thing you do when you're an adult, right? Throw dinner parties. Reminder that you can choose anyone throughout history for this one-off fancy feast. Here are my picks:

Abraham Lincoln

I don't really know what we would talk about, but how many people could say they hung out with ol' Abe over some tinned spaghetti and good times?

Pocahontas

She would come along to add a different element, she seems cool and spiritual.

Me when I was five

I was just so oblivious to everything going on around me at this age, I was pretty much just a little body walking around. I would just want to see me in action, but who would have my brain? Would I be old me or young me? Or both? Could we communicate telepathically? I hope to someday answer these very questions.

Barack Obama

He'd keep Abraham Lincoln happy when we ran out of things to talk about, and he'd owe me a favour afterwards for introducing them. I think it's a good idea to have a President on your favours list.

Anne Frank

She seems like a lovely girl, I'd love to see the way she looks at the world.

Actually, looking at this list now — everyone would have to bring their own food. I couldn't handle the pressure. I'd be eating saveloys in the corner with tomato sauce. It would be the weirdest party of all time.

My sort-of-achievable bucket list

Aside from all the horrible things that come with growing up like wine and not being allowed to wear ponchos, I'm also excited to keep working on my bucket list. Turns out that there are loads of other things I want to do aside from make burritos and become a world-famous Sandra Bullock stunt double. Here are five things that I want to tick off before I die due to getting eaten by a shark-zombie-chicken:

Go to Italy

It looks nice. I hope it's nice and not rubbish. You know how people can really talk a place up and then you get there and it smells and there are cats everywhere? I just want to eat a lot of fancy spaghetti bolognese, to be honest with you.

Get married

I'm not even picky as to who it is — I just want the fun ceremony. I've planned it out already in my head. It will be a small group of guests in a little wooden church. In the autumn. People will dress casually, but still cool. I won't wear my cowboy hat, put it that way. I really can see it all now: my closest friends and family standing between beautiful white pillars. Just need to put a face on that unidentified suit and tie.

Skydive

I am such a boring cliché, but I really feel like this is something you have to do once in your life. I'd be so scared the whole time, I'd definitely leave it till last on the list because I know for sure I would die either during or afterwards. Far out, my outlook on life is so depressing. I'm sorry.

Live to 100

Oh yeah, so I have to make it to 100 before I do the skydive that is sure to stop my heart. I really want to get one of those flash certificates from the Queen. Imagine how much the world will change in 100 years?! Hopefully my videos are completely invisible by then. This generation of YouTube will be like the archival classics on loop in museum foyers that no-one watches.

Meet Justin Bieber

I've already said he's my one of my all-time crushes; I'd like to see his impressive Rubik's Cube-solving skills in action. Did you know he could solve them even when he was younger? Man of many talents, I tell ya.

Jamie's end-of-book quiz

Remember at the start how I said you should pay attention because there was going to be a quiz at the end? Well, you should have taken me seriously, because here it is. Coming at you crazy fast, faster than me whizzing down the driveway with my umbrella and roller skates. Faster than a magpie coming to peck my head. Faster than you just put down this book.

Pens at the ready, let's see how much attention you were paying . . .

I passed so you should too

GOODLUCK!

Quiz questions

How did Dave Franco die in my dream?

(A: Exploding cigar.)

What did I sneak out of school to get?

(A: Tomato sauce.)

What toy did I hold on to in a store and essentially steal?

(A: Barney.)

How many hats is too many hats?

(A: One. I have 34.)

How many times did my parents say embarrassing things in this book?

(A: 900.)

How much milk do you use to make my special scones?

(A: Just a whole thing of milk.)

What YouTuber do I want to meet the most?

(A: Grace Helbig.)

What did I do wrong at work experience?

(A: Everything. Existed.)

Why did I start Jamie's World?

(A: To take the piss.)

Who have I been mistaken for four times?

(A: Lorde.)

What donuts do I get at the airport?

(A: Jelly and glazed.)

What's in the secret box?

(A: Wouldn't you like to know?)

How old was my seventh form ball dress?

(A: Archaeologists couldn't even tell you.)

Whose body double do I want to be?

(A: Sandra Bullock.)

What are the numerals in pi?

(A: 3.141592653589793238462643383279.)

What goes good on pi?

(A: Naughty tomato sauce.)

What's the scariest thing?

(A: A zombified shark with the head of a chicken and the nose of Pinocchio, trying to attack me 50 metres in the air.)

How many ChapSticks must I have on the go?

(A: Three.)

What is the point of a face mask?

(A: To burn off a layer of skin.)

Are high heels good?

(A: NO.)

Will I ever eat an oyster?

(A: Never in a million years, but thanks for playing.)

•••••••••••••••••••••••••••

How Do I End a Book if I Can't Even End a Video?

'WHEN YOU GET OUT INTO THE BIGGER WORLD, YOU REALISE THAT PEOPLE DON'T ACTUALLY CARE IF YOU ARE A TOTAL WEIRDO.'

WHAT HAVE I LEARNT FROM THIS CRAZY

ride so far? First of all, most of it hasn't been a ride —
I've spent most of my time sitting on my butt talking to a
camera. But I have learnt some things. I've learnt that the
world is really big. A lot bigger than Napier. I have met people all over the world, and I'm excited to have fancy global
friends everywhere now. I've learnt that there are a lot of
people just like me out there, and when you connect with
each other it's more exciting than any twist episode of *CSI*.

It's so weird to think back that I used to care so much
about what people in Napier, New Zealand thought about
me. When you get out into the bigger world, you realise
that people don't actually care if you are a total weirdo. In
fact, everyone's a bit of a weirdo in their own special way

'I COULD MOVE TO
LA AND TRY TO BE
A MOVIE STAR OR
I COULD STAY IN
NEW ZEALAND AND
FINALLY FULFIL
MY LIFELONG
DREAM OF BEING
A GARBAGE MAN.'

— from my own dad to the lady who thought I was Lorde to the person who sent me a watermelon. All a bunch of crazies. I've gained a lot more confidence in myself through Jamie's World, and I can only hope that people have seen something of themselves in my slip-ups, ramblings and way-too-high pants.

I don't know what's going to happen in the next chin chapters of my life. Who knows where I'll take my chins? I could move to LA and try to be a movie star or I could stay in New Zealand and finally fulfil my lifelong dream of being a garbage man. Maybe I'll fish out the racquets and get back into badminton. Whatever happens, I'd love it if you could stick around to see. Without getting too mushy, it's nice to know that there are weird chickens just like me all around the world.

'WITHOUT GETTING TOO MUSHY, IT'S NICE TO KNOW THAT THERE ARE WEIRD CHICKENS JUST LIKE ME ALL AROUND THE WORLD.'

My favourite saying is one from Dr Seuss, and I think sums up what I've been trying to say this whole time, and what I wish I knew when I was sitting in a hole wearing a cowboy hat:

'THOSE WHO MATTER DON'T MIND, AND THOSE WHO MIND DON'T MATTER.'

That's my favourite saying in the world. That and 'What's for dinner?' I couldn't decide which one was better to end on, so pick your favourite and run with it.

Here we go ... the awkward ending. Do we hug? Do we shake hands? Will you call me or will I call you? Shall we just see what happens? Well, the book is over now ... That's the book ... Done and dusted. All right ... Bye.

(Now would be a good time to clap the book shut like the clap at the end of my videos, but don't let me tell you how to live your life ...)

clap

Heyoooo! I hope you all enjoyed the book! If not, lol soz. But I just want to give a big thank you to all the people that made it happen. First a big thanks to Anna Lawrence and Imogen Johnson — my two main homies at Johnson & Laird Management (J&L). Thank you for keeping me motivated to get this done. And a big thanks to the rest of the team at J&L. Thank you to Alex Casey! This girl right here was my book wingman. Thanks for putting up with me and my poor writing skills. The book wouldn't have made sense without you! Thanks, Finlay Macdonald at HarperCollins, for this opportunity! Has been soooo sick! Never thought in a million years I'd have a book but there ya go. And thank you to everyone else involved! I could go on forever but you know who you are! And one last huuuge thank you to you guys! Thanks for watching my videos and liking my pointless photos in Instagram. All the support you guys give me is amazing and hasn't gone unnoticed.

Jamie x